Symbolic Domination

Paul Rabinow

Symbolic Domination

Cultural Form and Historical Change in Morocco

The University of Chicago Press
Chicago and London

The photographs reproduced in this volume
are by Paul Hyman.

The University of Chicago Press, Chicago 60637
The University of Chicago Press, Ltd., London

Library of Congress Cataloging in Publication Data

Rabinow, Paul.
   Symbolic domination.

   1. Zaouia Sidi Lahsene, Morocco.   2. Islam—Zaouia Sidi
Lahsene, Morocco.   3. Morocco—Civilization.
4. Morocco—Politics.   I. Title.
DT329.Z36R3   301.29'64   74-7565
ISBN 0-226-70149-2 pbk.

Contents

To Abdelkrim
Mohammed
Chef Abdelkrim
Omar
Ali
for their hospitality

Acknowledgments

My thanks go first of all to the Moroccans and particularly to the people of Sidi Lahcen who put up with my seemingly irrelevant questions and presence.

My second debt is to Clifford Geertz, whose advice, maturely tempered and restrained, allowed me to proceed on my own during both the fieldwork and writing. His on-going support, sprinkled with moments of doubt, yielded a productive tension (for both, I hope).

I am grateful to the National Institute of Mental Health for supporting my graduate education and fieldwork, and to the Institute for Advanced Study in Princeton, where most of the book was written.

Particular thanks are due to the enormously generous efforts of Elizabeth Friedman, Hildred Geertz, Paul Hyman, and Toby Volkman, who gave the text whatever readability it has.

An intellectual debt is owed to Steven Barnett, Pierre Bourdieu, Edmund Burke, Elizabeth Friedman, Clifford and Hildred Geertz, Paul Hyman, Kenneth Maxwell, Sherry Ortner, and James Siegel for many hours of helpful discussions.

Many thanks to Paul Hyman for the use of his photographs and for the insights they provide.

Thanks to the secretaries at the Institute, Anna Marie Holt and Catherine Rhubart, who did most of the typing.

The fieldwork which forms the basis of this book was carried out during 1968–69. Much of the specific ethnographic detail, which would otherwise be found here, has been purposively pruned. This essential background will be covered in a forthcoming ethnography of the Sefrou area, by myself, Lawrence Rosen, and Clifford and Hildred Geertz.

Note on Transliteration

No attempt is˘ made to present a phonetically accurate system of transliteration in this book. The reason for this is twofold. First, there is no standardized system for Moroccan Arabic; the literature is full of idiosyncratic variants. Second, the economics of the publishing industry today makes even a modest attempt at accuracy financially prohibitive. Therefore, I have tried to give transliterations which are consistent within the book. They should also enable the reader to identify names, places and terms. I believe that the Arabic words will be recognizable to those who speak Moroccan.

Illustrations

Morocco at the Time of Sidi Lahcen

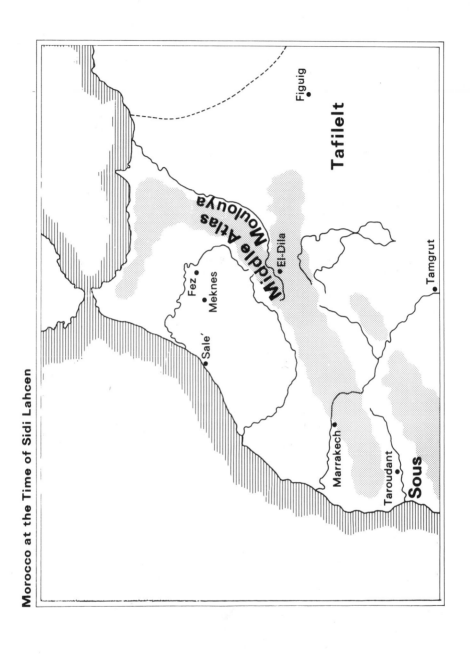

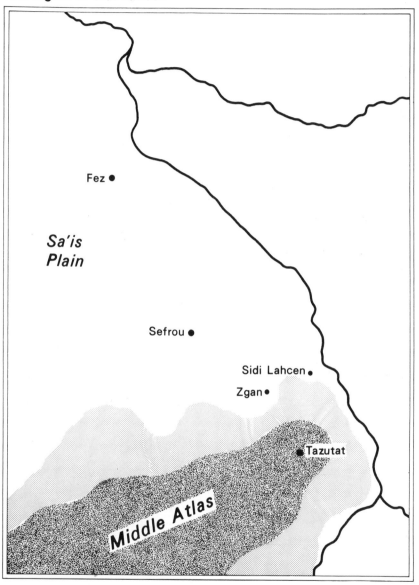

The Village of Sidi Lahcen

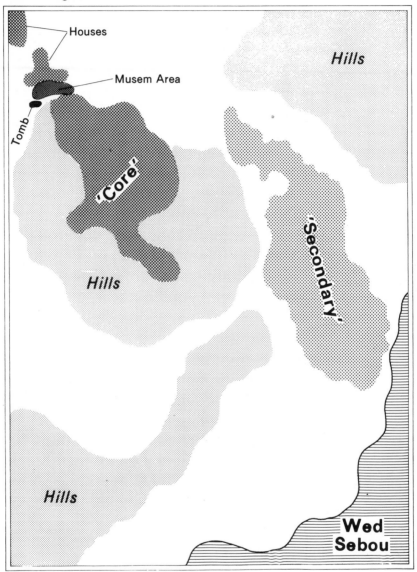

1. Not even a shepherd

2. Chef Abdel Krim: *"Les grosses têtes jamais la-bas"*

1

2

3. With limited possibilities . . .

4. Ali in his store

5. The children of the wlad abad were
separated from the children of the wlad
siyyed

4

5

6. A modern wlad abad and his family
visit the village on market day:
defiance is not without its tensions

7. The Ait Ghazi ben Allal: the rewards
of solidarity

6

7

8. Ali and a member of the wlad
siyyed: deceptive laughter

9. The musem

10. *Ila mandek-sh l-flus, klam-ek messus*, "With no money, your words are bitter"

9

10

11. An **almost** paralytic anxiety...

11

Introduction

Tradition
and
Alienation

Tradition is a moving image of the past. When a culture stops moving, when its structures of belief no longer offer a means to integrate, create, and make meaningful new experiences, then a process of alienation begins. Tradition is opposed not to modernity but to alienation.

As conditions alter, symbols change their meaning even if the literal sense remains constant. Cultural meaning and coherence always exist in relative association with a general historical situation, never in themselves. Parts of a tradition may wither and die while others continue to move and flourish. Alienation consists in the attempt to maintain a fixed sense of symbols once other conditions have shifted. Claims of generalized validity based on older self-definitions raise the stakes of emotional commitment to what was, and lessen the chances of rejuvenation. The process builds over relatively long stretches of time, and self-consciousness of its course occurs near the end. When a group finally comprehends itself to be in the throes of this process, it is often too late to do much but suffer or rage.[1]

Our specific concern is with a group of religious leaders in the Middle Atlas mountains of Morocco who are descendants of a famous seventeenth-century saint, Sidi Lahcen Lyussi, renowned for his erudition and religious power. Until the establishment of the French Protectorate in 1912, the descendants were considered to be guardians and possessors of that power. Today, they describe themselves as "withered grapes on the great vine of Sidi Lahcen."

It is important to stress that this account is *not* a discussion of how modernity destroys tradition. The terms are not necessarily opposed.

In fundamental ways, Moroccan culture is still very much alive and continues to provide a meaningful framework for interpreting the world. The vine, to continue the metaphor, is still flourishing for many Moroccans. The descendants of the saint, however, find themselves estranged. This group and its problems are not unique in Morocco. Culture neither changes in quantum jumps, nor simultaneously across a whole society. Rather, change—and particularly cultural change—occurs slowly, partially, at different rates for different groups and individuals, and in different forms. Particular groups and individuals attempt to incorporate, interpret, and go beyond new situations which are imposed on them or which they themselves have created. Some are more successful than others.

Imperialism has forced the problem of tradition and alienation on the world (the West, of course, included) in a violent form. In some areas, the impact of imperialist and colonial expansion has been so drastic and long-lasting that even social, economic, and cultural structures must be defined in terms of a reaction to colonial expansion. In Algeria, for example, the French carried out systematic policies aimed at destroying traditional (or what they thought to be traditional) social and economic structures and were largely successful. Many groups in Algeria were forced to choose between an almost complete assimilation of French culture or a defensive and embattled Islam. Domination on all levels over an extended period was the given.

In Morocco the situation was rather different. Dislocation and domination were much less severe than in Algeria. The occupation was some ninety years shorter, there was neither massive colonization nor systematic destruction of local social and economic structures, and the winning of independence was significantly less destructive and bloody.

Morocco had had a more highly integrated culture and polity before European expansion. Because the imperialist onslaught was less drastic than in Algeria, a situation was created in which a wide range of responses was possible. Indeed, a great variety of economic, religious, and social reactions occurred.

These historical particularities—the somewhat late impact of colonialism and the vitality of the culture—combine to highlight the contours of this generalized historical phenomenon. *Baraka*, the central symbol of vitality in Moroccan culture, still gives force to the vine, even though the French have pruned it. Certain grapes, however, are dried, withered, and tired. Whether the vine itself will endure remains to be seen. In any case, the Moroccan religious situation is a great deal more vigorous than its economic one.

In the case of the saint's descendants, a particular set of their own actions has choked off the baraka which once sustained them. By clinging to self-definitions and by interpreting new possibilities in a very circumscribed and limited way—in the name of what they considered to be their highest values and in defense of their cultural identity—they have succeeded in undermining the very cultural identity they were seeking to preserve. In other terms, by reifying certain symbols, they initiated a process of alienation; these very symbols, which once provided a vital source of their cultural identity, have now come to haunt this group. By holding themselves in a position in which they cannot be traditional because new political, economic and ecological conditions now prevail, they have defined themselves into a corner and they know it. This is not the result of a necessary process of the conflict of the pan-historical forces of tradition and modernity. Other groups in the region have not undergone this same process. The rural Berbers who come to the village to celebrate the saint's festival find the symbols very much alive—potent vehicles through which they can integrate new conditions. They have not stopped moving. For them, Moroccan Islam is contemporary. Ironically, for the *wlad siyyed*, the guardians of the saint's baraka, religion is becoming self-consciously traditional.

The method I employ is actor-oriented and what has been called progressive-regressive.[2] An actor-oriented method attempts to understand the actor's view of his own social world. It involves analysis of the symbols which give meaning and through which understanding is possible, as well as the social and economic conditions within which these symbols operate; in other words, how experience is organized.

Symbolic analysis must also be historically oriented. Cultural symbols do not think themselves or play out their own codes; they exist in time, in particular societies, and they develop or disappear. Their meaning is made historically concrete through action. Central symbols are highly ambiguous, expressive, and inherently susceptible to many interpretations; this is what makes them central. To understand the present state of a set of core symbols in a culture one must first move regressively backward to trace their development. One tries to isolate these symbols and situate them within particular social and historical conditions from which they arose and to which they gave meaning. This process is always somewhat arbitrary. In principle one could extend it back to any point in time. In practice this is rarely a problem. Where to stop is guided by the material itself and the questions one is asking of that material. In our case, we can point to the severe and prolonged crisis which Moroccan society underwent from the fifteenth to the seventeenth centuries, which was finally resolved with the emergence and stabilization of a new dynasty.

We focus on local communities because it is here that new economic conditions have their most marked effect, religious movements find their adherents, raw materials are extracted, political leaders find their followers. Basic social and cultural changes may be initiated elsewhere, but it is on the local scene that change is integrated and interpreted if it is to have social import. Therefore an analysis of social change must move from worldwide shifts through a series of mediations to national, regional, and even individual changes, and then back again into broader integrations. If we are to understand social change, we must attempt this accordionlike expansion and contraction both vertically in terms of time and horizontally in terms of space.

There certainly has been sufficient discussion within anthropology to demonstrate that men are born into a world which is already formed, that they are socialized into it and perceive reality in terms of the categories which their elders have passed on to them. What has rarely been stressed, however, is that they also act. Although men do not fully gauge the implications of their acts, and the consequences often escape and return to haunt them, it is still men, not social systems, who produce social action.

As observers of another culture, we cannot negate our presence as outsiders, nor do we wish to. Our cultural distance provides us with an external vantage point from which we can see and understand certain results, unintended consequences, and the weight of past circumstances in the lives of the people we are observing. But the fact that men do not fully comprehend or consciously make their own history, and that, for the most part, it eludes their understanding and control, does not mean that they are not their own self-product. Man objectifies and often alienates himself in history. His own actions appear alien to the extent that, as social action occurs, he neither understands nor internalizes the larger totalities.

Man is a self-product of his own past as well as a prisoner of it. He lives amid his own self-definitions, largely passed down to him or imposed on him. These parameters are neither static nor simply external. They are always partially integrated and internalized. General cultural symbols and structures are made particular through man's actions.

1. Sidi Lahcen and His Age

*The Emergence
of the
Sherifian Sultanate*

Morocco in 1605 was in a state of general disorder. The central power was crumbling rapidly and the countryside was filled with charismatic holy men seeking to build political movements. By 1675, Morocco had a strong central government ruled by an enigmatic, brutal, and powerful Sultan, a descendant of the Prophet Mohammed. In the beginning of the century, charismatic leadership carried the day; by the end of the century, both in the central government and in the remaining religious brotherhoods, hereditary, genealogical leadership had established itself, and it still prevails today.[1] By the end of the seventeenth century, the religious brotherhoods with political ambitions had been demolished, and the others were under close surveillance, maintaining their independence at the price of symbolic submission and political neutrality.

Since the eleventh and twelfth centuries, when the Berber kingdoms of the Almoravids and Almohads had unified Morocco on the basis of reformist zeal and powerful military organization, there had been no dynasty which had been able to establish and sustain a powerful, central control or a principle of on-going legitimacy.[2] Periods of relative consolidation were followed by periods marked by disorder; no enduring political institutions emerged, and no basis of political legitimacy was forged.

This failure became crucial in the fifteenth century, when the European maritime powers began to appear on Morocco's shores, shaking the country deeply and bringing her self-conception as a Muslim realm into question.[3] The mere presence of the Christians, not to mention their military superiority, was deeply humiliating to

Morocco both religiously and politically and was to have profound effects in both realms. Symbolic submission and the passionate reaction to it have been a main theme in Moroccan history.

Portuguese influence reached its peak during the second half of the fifteenth century when Portugal controlled not only ports but several inland areas in a kind of protectorate relationship. The Portuguese incursions stemmed from larger imperialistic aims; they wanted ports, wheat, animals, and trade from Morocco. The Saharan gold trade, which had been a cornerstone of the Moroccan economy throughout the Middle Ages, now shifted to the coastal routes established by the Portuguese. This brought temporary prosperity, but in the long run the shift (and the growing importance of the Turks in the east) minimized the economic role of the gold trade for Morocco.

The Portuguese and Spanish incursions, coincident with the expulsion of Muslims from Andalusia, had deep religious overtones even if the primary motivation was economic. Inside Morocco the response to the incursions took a religious form and opened a period of religious and political turmoil that was not to be calmed for two hundred years. The reaction was led by partisan holy men and the heads of the increasingly important Sufi brotherhoods.

The direct threat of the Portuguese diminished rather abruptly during the sixteenth century as they turned their attention and energies elsewhere. Yet Morocco's problems continued. Urban life declined and the economy contracted. The economic failure was matched by the continuing inability of the various groups to achieve a forceful political form. The leader of the Beni Wattsid dynasty referred to himself as *sheikh* of the kingdom.[4] This tribal term, meaning "leader," indicates the limited scope of political ideas then current.

The continued agitation of the Sufi brotherhoods and of individual saints marked the religious scene. During the second half of the sixteenth century, however, an element of great importance emerged with the appearance of the Saadian *shurfa* in the south. This group used its claim of descent from the Prophet as a legitimating principle, differentiating it from most other religiously led groups. For a time, the Saadians did manage to ride the crest of the holy war and achieve dynastic power. The principle of sherifian descent became an important aspect of the religious-political arena in Morocco. After a brief period of successful rule, however, their power failed. The reemergence of the Portuguese combined with internal problems to throw Morocco once again into crisis.

Warrior saints, holy men, zealots, and miracle workers began to rally the tribes against the infidels and the Saadian government's failure to drive them out. The so-called "Maraboutic (or Saint) Crisis" was underway. Politically, the crisis entailed. the dissolution of the remaining central power, the emergence of a large number of sectarian communities led by charismatic figures, the consolidation of these religious-political groups into several large, competing "confederacies," and the eventual triumph of the Alawite shurfa, descendants of the Prophet Mohammed, from the Tafilelt region. The Alawites finally succeeded in crushing the other politically important communities and establishing themselves as the ruling dynasty, a position they still hold today. Emerging from the swirl of fragmented, competing, sectarian groups, the Alawites molded a strong, centralized, legitimate institution, the Sultanate, which since the mid-seventeenth century has been one of the poles of the Moroccan political order. Its influence, power, and style have varied greatly, but its fundamental legitimacy has not been successfully challenged. All other political groups in Morocco have had to define their relationship to the Alawite sultan. Although the relationship has changed, the basic political order created by the Alawites has survived.

The Maraboutic Crisis and its resolution through the triumph of the Alawites also wrought a basic new form for the religious order in Morocco. The religious crisis turned on a conflict between two sources of religious power and authority: the hereditary or genealogical, and the charismatic or miraculous. Both had existed as potent sources of authority in Morocco for many centuries. Saint worship is a fundamental and archaic institution in North Africa. Further, the emergence of either of these sources of authority as a catalyst for political movements in Morocco was an ancient and common occurrence. What was new was the scope, the "luxuriance of political expression"[5] which religious figures commanded and the fact that by the mid-seventeenth century the two principles and the corresponding political movements were clearly opposed to one another.

Various extraordinary individuals were seen as having divine powers; they were seen as exemplifying God's grace on earth. Communities of followers gathered around them to share in their divine power. Those communities which attempted to transform this personal (or charismatic) religious force into a political form flourished during the Maraboutic Crisis, but were finally destroyed by the success of the Alawites.

The other principle, that of hereditary transmission of religious power and authority, was the one that prevailed. This is not to say that the personal, miraculous source was eliminated; quite the contrary. But it was subordinated to and institutionalized through a hereditary mode of transmission: namely, the descendants of particularly holy men (the Prophet Mohammed being the holiest) were now seen as more likely to possess religious power and authority than those lacking genealogical connections. Thus, in each generation several (or one or even none) of the descendants of a particular saint will receive his baraka, his religious power, becoming the guardian of it and, thereby, of the group's interests. When he or she dies, someone else will succeed as the possessor of the saint's baraka. The original source of the baraka was charismatic and individual, and its current manifestation might also be, but the principle of transmission was now hereditary or, better, genealogical. Baraka was seen to flow along genealogical lines. Thus, in any particular generation there might be no descendants who were considered to be men of baraka; the baraka still inhered in the genealogical line connecting them to the saint or Prophet, and it might manifest itself more strongly in the next generation. This was especially true for the *shurfa*, or descendants of the Prophet Mohammed. Their genealogical attachment to the Prophet predisposed them to have certain powers and to be more holy than the non-shurfa. With the success of the Alawites, this conception gained a centrality and importance it had never had before. The Sultanate was now not only a consequential political role but it was a religious one as well. The sultan was a *sherif*, adding a second source of authority and legitimacy to the position, and giving added support and prestige to all the shurfa in Morocco. Obviously not every sultan had personal charisma, but every sultan was an Alawite sherif. A new order with its own potent symbols had been introduced.

A parallel process was occurring among saints' descendants. Since not every saint was a sherif, many of the descendants sought added baraka by having their ancestor declared sherif. They could do this by obtaining a decree from the sultan legitimating their credentials.[6] So an increased religious centralization occurred through the establishment and institutionalization of the Alawite shurfa and through their control of the official legitimating symbols. There was an interplay here, which we will also see in the political realm, of the central authorities reinforcing what had already established itself on the local level, and local figures seeking symbolic support from the central authorities to further consolidate (or shore up) their own position. What was established, therefore, was a concurrence on an institution and its symbols. Obviously, the Alawites had no monopoly on divine grace (saint worship continued to flourish throughout their reign, albeit without the same political consequences), nor were all of the Alawite rulers charismatic, but a consensus on the symbols of religious power and its mode of transmission gave Morocco the basis for a cultural continuity which has lasted three hundred years.

To examine some of the implications and dynamics of this particular form and its development, we turn first to two prominent seventeenth-century religious brotherhoods. The styles and destinies of these orders can be seen as epitomizing, in an ideal typical sense, the fates and choices which faced Moroccan society during this period of turmoil and emergent order. In a sense, they represent the two poles of the relation of religious power to political power within Moroccan society. I use this portrayal to set the scene for the introduction of Sidi Lahcen Lyussi. This saint had intimate contact with both of the brotherhoods, as well as with the Alawites who subdued them all. The story presented here illustrates a range of responses to a particular historical situation. Some of these responses were more successful than others. The technique of exemplification and structural variation will be employed throughout. We turn first to a northern brotherhood that combined religious excellence with political ambition.

EL-DILA

The *zawiya* of el-Dila was founded in the middle of the sixteenth century. Zawiya refers to the lodge where a Sufi mystic brotherhood gathered. This particular zawiya had a modest origin and during its early years was concerned entirely with scholarly activity and mystical pursuits. Its founder, a Sendhaja Berber, achieved a local reputation for his piety, erudition, and indifference to worldly goods. Despite such humble beginnings, this brotherhood during the course of little more than a century was to conquer most of northern Morocco. It fell even more rapidly.

Having no political ambitions initially, the brotherhood was able to grow and consolidate at its own pace. The leaders of the brotherhood willingly submitted to the political and spiritual authority of the Saadians as well as to the warrior saint who was leading the fight against the Portuguese.

As so often happens in Morocco, however, great spiritual power brings wealth along with it, leading to political ambition. As the religious importance of el-Dila grew, the Berber tribes surrounding the lodge began pledging their military and political allegiances, repeating "that easy miracle that one observes at the beginning of each zawiya of spreading liberally to some what one has received from others,"[7] namely, wealth. The Berber tribes of the Middle Atlas united under the new leader of the zawiya, Sidi Mohammed l-Hajj, who, unlike his predecessors, eagerly sought and encouraged the temporal support of the tribes.

The spiritual reputation of el-Dila also reached its peak in these years, and it became perhaps the most famous center of learning in Morocco. "Night and day, the students gave themselves to the pursuit of science, and the courses continued without interruption. A large number of masters and thinkers were produced by the zawiya. Students came from every corner of Morocco, and none who was eager to learn would consider going anywhere else."[8]

In an atmosphere of crumbling central power, el-Dila made its first aggressive move to the south. This was a testing thrust directed against the other main religious-political community, the Alawite shurfa in Tafilelt. The two religious powers, realizing that neither was strong enough to eliminate the other, agreed on a temporary truce which secured el-Dila's southern flank and freed them for a move against the Saadians. The key battle took place on the rich wheat-growing Sais plain outside of Fez, and el-Dila soundly defeated the sultan's forces, thereby winning control of the key positions in northern Morocco.

This victory, in 1646, marked the height of el-Dila's power. The brotherhood had secured a hold in the south, and controlled the main power centers in the north, Fez, Salé, the key port in Morocco, and the rich agricultural land which lay between them.

This consolidation was short-lived. Characteristically, local rebellions began to appear, even in the Middle Atlas heartlands; the patchwork nature of the confederation became evident. While these internal dissensions were occurring, the Alawites went on the offensive. Coming out of their southern base at Tafilelt, they captured Fez, aided by internal uprisings. From Fez, they challenged el-Dila, met its members in battle and thoroughly routed them as many tribes abruptly abandoned the brotherhood. In 1668, el-Dila was definitively beaten. The lodge was sacked, its buildings were demolished (to such an extent that scholars still debate its exact location), its leaders exiled, and its fields covered with salt.

El-Dila represents one of the last attempts of a Sufi brotherhood to achieve national power. It stands at a pole of Moroccan social life where religious power is parlayed directly into political power. This was not the last time that a religious brotherhood would achieve political importance in Moroccan history. But it was the last time that the attempt was so total and successful even for a short period. From the defeat of el-Dila on, brotherhoods would continue to have influence in Morocco, but they no longer would produce dynasties or rulers.

THE ZAWIYA AT TAMGRUT

We turn now to the south. Here we encounter another prominent brotherhood. In this case, however, religious prominence was combined with careful and artful avoidance of political challenge to the central government. Political ambition was confined to the local arena. This response proved to be paradigmatic of the attitude which Moroccan brotherhoods would adopt after this. Henceforth, religious prominence at a national level would be carefully used to influence the national government, but the consolidation of political power would be possible only at the local level.

The Draa River valley in the deep southwest of Morocco had fallen into a state of disorder by the end of the sixteenth century. The rise of the highly moral, rigorously puritanical, and scholarly leaders at Tamgrut signaled the appearance of a new authority in the region. By dint of their exemplary moral characters, the first leaders of the brotherhood at Tamgrut were soon called upon to play an important mediation role for the warring tribes. As their spiritual reputation and influence increased, they were able not only to arbitrate specific disputes but to call for and achieve periodic truces. This helped restore the economic life of the region. They also played a role in protecting the caravan trade.

Naturally, this protection was paid for, swelling the coffers of the Tamgrut lodge, which proceeded, as had el-Dila, to redistribute the wealth among the tribes in the region. Tamgrut's ascendancy began around the year 1635, when the grandson of its founder came to power. A great scholar, he was also a holy man, famous for many miracles.

The leadership of the brotherhood passed after his death not to this man's son but rather to his best pupil, Sidi Mohammed ben Nasr, whose knowledge and simple piety were already legendary. His fame spread over the south, drawing many students and helping to establish Tamgrut as an important religious center. Sidi Mohammed himself lived in poverty. All the goods that he collected he turned over to the lodge. His modesty was renowned and his spiritual reputation and power grew. Sidi Mohammed preached a puritanical doctrine and actively combated what to him were the pagan practices of the tribesmen—singing, dancing, smoking.

Sidi Mohammed's virtue and naïveté led him to place the interest of his kin behind those of the brotherhood. His kin hatched a plot against him and he was forced to flee the lodge. He eventually resolved the dilemma between hereditary claimants and spiritual heirs by marrying one of his teacher's daughters, thus tying himself to the hereditary owners of the land. He gave them control over the benefits from the brotherhood, which appeased them and freed him to pursue his spiritual aims. He spent the next thirty years, 1645–75, studying and teaching.

A crisis was avoided for the zawiya by the fortunate coincidence that Sidi Mohammed's son was also his leading disciple. In the next two generations hereditary and personal charisma were fused, but in the long run hereditary transmission of holiness predominated here as well.

Sidi Mohammed's politics were simple in principle—he advocated a strict neutrality—but very complex and delicate in application. He refused to enter into any formal agreements with the central government or even to pronounce the name of the sultan in the Friday prayer, an act of defiance. Even when the Alawite dynasty came to power, he defended his continuing refusal to pronounce the sultan's name by saying that in Sunni doctrine all believers were equal.

His son continued this policy of political neutrality and independence, again refusing to pronounce the name of the Alawite sultan in the Friday prayer. By this point, however, the Alawites were in the final stages of consolidating their political control over Morocco. The sultan Moulay Ismail was particularly attentive to the dissident religious brotherhoods and worked systematically at their submission. To this end, Moulay Ismail summoned the leader of the Tamgrut brotherhood to the new imperial capital at Meknes. The sultan is supposed to have said upon meeting the religious leader: "When I held his hand in mine, mine trembled. By this I recognize his firm attachment to Allah and that his sole concern is with religion. Other saints' hands trembled in mine because they were concerned with this world."[9] Neutrality and independence were thus maintained by the power of the saint's piety. But the saint's mere presence in the sultan's court was itself a tacit agreement to render unto Caesar that which is Caesar's. Neutrality and independence now meant "with the consent of the Alawites and solely for religious ends." The brotherhood has maintained this stance of devotion to local mediation and to scholarly matters since that time, and, although somewhat impoverished, it is still an active center of religious activity in the south.

We turn next to Sidi Lahcen Lyussi, who lived and studied with both of these brotherhoods.

SIDI LAHCEN LYUSSI: WANDERING SCHOLAR AND SAINT

Sidi Lahcen Lyussi,[10] whose real name was Abu Ali Lahcen ben Masud, was born in 1631 among the Berber tribes of the Haute Moulouya, after the foundation but approximately coincident with the maturation of the two scholastic religious centers, el-Dila and Tamgrut. He grew up among tribes whose transhumance patterns were being threatened by the rise of political powers both to the south (Alawites) and, more importantly, to the north, where the imperial forces of the Saadians were extending their control through the Sais plain to the edges of the Middle Atlas. In part, the rise of the el-Dila brotherhood was a defensive response to this pressure.

Sidi Lahcen tells us in his autobiography that he was precocious. Having quickly surpassed the teachers at the local mosque, he left home in search of both spiritual and intellectual knowledge. He never really settled down. He wandered from brotherhood to brotherhood, from saint's tomb to saint's tomb, living on the charity of the pious. This hard and uncertain life tested and formed the character of the wandering student in seventeenth-century Morocco.

Still quite young, he traveled south to Marrakech and the Sous, where he first gained his scholarly reputation through the agility of his dialectic and the scope of his knowledge. His abilities so impressed a local prince that he was rewarded, though only eighteen, with a teaching post at Taroudant. The awarding of this type of position was based on personal authority and presence, which must have been truly unusual in the case of Sidi Lahcen. However, he left the post in 1650, after only one year, and continued farther south to Tamgrut, where he became a disciple of Sidi Mohammed ben Nasr.

His stay at Tamgrut was a happy if arduous one. Fervent involvement was demanded of the students; he often went without sleep for days on end. Jacques Berque characterizes Sidi Lahcen's spiritual state at Tamgrut as "many long periods of drought watered by sudden illuminations,"[11] eased by the reverence for the great masters who were his teachers.

Although he left Tamgrut later that year, he often returned to visit his master, Sidi Mohammed. His humility before the master, he tells us in his autobiography, was so great that he was ashamed even to stand in his presence.

Sidi Lahcen returned to northern Morocco, where he settled at el-Dila for fifteen years of study and contemplation. These years, from 1653 to 1668, proved to be the longest period of stability in his life. As we have seen, this was a period of decisive political change in

Morocco; in 1668, el-Dila was smashed by the Alawites. Although the brotherhood was totally destroyed, Sidi Lahcen escaped its fate, having successfully avoided identification with its leaders.

Sidi Lahcen left with the Alawites, and returned to Fez with the grant of a teaching position. His course at the Qarawiyin mosque attracted large audiences including, it is said, the sultan Moulay Rachid. Sidi Lahcen was now among the most respected scholars in Fez, the intellectual and political capital of Morocco. He never settled permanently there, however; it is unclear whether this was by his own choice or because of the Fassi hostility to this Berber savant. We do know that his stay there was marked by polemical attacks and counterattacks. The popularity of his courses caused much envy in this urbane capital.

In 1672, near anarchy compounded by an economic crisis produced great uncertainty in Morocco and particularly in Fez, where open rebellion broke out. Shortly before the rebellion, Sidi Lahcen had left for a tour of saints' tombs in the far north, leaving Fez to its politics and thereby escaping the harsh retaliation taken on the city by the sultan Moulay Ismail.

Briefly returning to Fez and finding it still in a state of disorder, Sidi Lahcen sent a famous letter to the sultan warning him against the abuse of his power. This act was all the more surprising given the mutual antagonism which existed between the Fassis and the saint. The audacity and sagacity of the latter so impressed the sultan that he invited Sidi Lahcen to his court in Meknes. Sidi Lahcen was bold enough to refuse the offer, although it does seem that he passed through Meknes long enough to claim his credentials as a sherif. Little is known about the end of his life, but a legend claims that he retired to the Middle Atlas Mountains to preach to the Berbers. In any case, he was purportedly buried there in 1691.

His life was one of restless and nearly constant movement. Through his travels Sidi Lahcen came to know and love the whole fragmented and warring kingdom which was soon to be united under the Alawite dynasty. He studied with the great masters of his day: high in the mountains with the politically ambitious and expansionist brotherhood of el-Dila, which he saw destroyed; deep in the pre-Saharan austerity of Tamgrut with his true master and guide, the saint Mohammed ben Nasr; in the great urban centers, both of the south (Marrakech and Taroudant), where he established his initial intellectual and spiritual reputation, and in the traditional center of the north, Fez, where he held his own against the renowned doctors of his day and established and then abandoned his position at the imperial court.

He also visited hundreds of minor brotherhoods found alongside the hundreds of saints' tombs all over the kingdom, where he passed many nights hearing tales of miraculous cures and legendary genealogies.

Sidi Lahcen was a poet, jurist, theologian, polemicist, logician, and autobiographer. His dialectical skills, especially his synthetic and appreciative abilities, were highly praised by his contemporaries, and his works are still read in Morocco. He has left an autobiography, *Muhadarat*, an almost unique document in Moroccan literature. Confronting the disparity between the orthodox Muslim principle of the equality of believers and the inequalities that were so apparent in Morocco, Sidi Lahcen held the position—then being undermined— that only personal nobility could be the source of inequality. That nobility, as Sidi Lahcen discerned it, might be found in the ascetic, scholarly purity of Mohammed ben Nasr, or, at the other extreme, occasionally it might be found among certain of the popular saints. He hesitated to condemn popular worship categorically; he would not go along with the systematic destruction of saints' tombs that some theological extremists advocated. He mused on the power of saint worship to satisfy the legitimate desires of the people. He visited many tombs, listened to the stories, and collected the genealogies of the saints. "Even in the worst epochs, when the content has practically disappeared, the names still exist and are piously collected. They alone feed the need for erudition, which has scarcely any worth except the preservation of a tradition and solidarity but continues to be worthwhile for this reason."[12] This shell was what Sidi Lahcen discovered in his wanderings north and south in Morocco, and he worked not so much to destroy it (as some of the Tamgrut purists wanted), or to despise it (as was the fashion in Fez), or unequivocally to vaunt it (as the many thousand pilgrims to the shrines did), as to revivify the tradition and to rejuvenate the basic religious spirit which had once animated it.

There was a blend in Sidi Lahcen of intuitive poetic insight coupled with the rigor of the dogmatist. He ridiculed the scholastic sterilities of the cities, but he himself wrote treatises on logic. When he found excesses of saint worship, such as in Tafilelt where he chopped down a tree that the villagers thought was holy so as to demonstrate that only Allah was divine, he sought to temper it while still defending the basis of popular religion. He studied with a mystic saint who preached Sunni orthodoxy and lived in an "atmosphere of miracles." His search was for the just mean. Berque sees this blend, this rigorous tolerance, as originating in his Berber background, which he never fully rejected nor could totally accept. His basic belief was in Islam and in the people of Morocco. Only after affirming these would he pass judgment on their current manifestations. He preached introspection and reveled in diversity.

During his lifetime, Sidi Lahcen knew four dynasties, or would-be dynasties, of which three were destroyed. He was keenly aware of the tenuousness of earthly kingdoms and refused them his confidence: "Three things elude confidence; the sea, time, the prince."[13] He lived during a period of decay and dissolution, but also one of emerging order, new form. The current prince, Sidi Lahcen maintained, was at best a temporal accident with whom the saint had to come to terms in order to achieve other goals; for the price of his silence, if not his fidelity, he was free to pursue his religion, his studies—even to be respected and consulted.

At the end of his life, Sidi Lahcen wrote two more letters to Moulay Ismail in which he forcefully reminded the sultan of the limits of his position, his subordination to Allah. He again warned the sultan against arrogance and the abuse of power. Yet he also demanded and received a *dahir*, decree, from the sultan testifying to his legitimate status as a sherif. The Berber savant made his bow to the new authority of the Alawite shurfa. Despite his wit, erudition, eloquence, and bravado, he acknowledged, by his act, the supremacy of the authority of the Alawite shurfa. On attaining this legitimacy, and again admonishing the sultan on the necessary separation of the religious realm from the political, he returned to the Middle Atlas mountains. A student of many great saints and scholars, Sidi Lahcen himself had few students, even fewer distinguished ones; but he did have many descendants.

2. The Legend of Sidi Lahcen

A Claim of
Legitimate Domination

Sidi Lahcen is said to be buried in a large, green-tiled tomb in the mountain village which bears his name. His descendants, the *wlad* Sidi Lahcen, claim his baraka, his divine grace, as their inheritance. Before the Protectorate they were active religious mediators for the Berber tribes in the region, and even though this function has been severely eroded, they are still the protectors of the saint's tomb and the guardians of his baraka. While they do not know[1] (nor are they concerned with) the historical details of their progenitor's life, they do have a legend about him.

Sefrou is a neighboring city of Sidi Lahcen some thirty kilometers away. The villagers go there to the market every week. Although the townspeople of Sefrou recognize the wlad Sidi Lahcen as descendants of a great saint, very few of them know even the most elemental versions of his legend. Even the members of the Ait Yussi tribe, the Berbers who come to the village to celebrate the saint twice a year, can recount little beyond the fact that Sidi Lahcen was a great scholar and a man of considerable baraka.

However, I found that within the village of Sidi Lahcen there existed a fairly uniform and succinct set of stories about the saint. Almost anyone in the village could repeat the main episodes of the legend, and almost no one from the outside seemed to know them. Further, within the village itself there was little variation from rendering to rendering.

No one faction outlined the legend in greater detail; it is not esoteric knowledge, or the property of a single group. The descendants of the saint gave substantially the same versions as the other villagers. In sum, the legend is commonly held, standardized, and restricted to the village as a whole. There are no ritual occasions on which it is recited, and it is rarely if ever presented sequentially as a whole.

The legend is composed of discrete sections or incidents, each focusing on particular, fundamentally important symbols. In each incident we are told a story which turns on a key religious symbol—baraka (divine grace), sherif-hood (descent from the prophet), etc. If we take the legend as a whole, we have an extensive (if unelaborate) gloss on the symbols which formulate the religious order on which the cultural identity of the saint's descendants is founded. That these symbols are central in Moroccan culture and are shared by the non-*wlad* inhabitants of Sidi Lahcen would not be disputed. How well the *wlad siyyed*, Sidi Lahcen's descendants, exemplify them certainly would be a subject of debate, intense debate at that.

The legend can also be read as a cultural geography of the region which situates the descendants of the saint. Finally, it can be seen as making a claim for legitimate domination by the wlad siyyed over the villagers who are not descendants of the saint. There certainly would be no disagreement that saints have baraka or that the sultan is a sherif. There would be no disagreement that the village of Sidi Lahcen is the religious center of the Ait Yussi tribe and that his tomb has more baraka than the other tombs in the region. But today the claim of inherent superiority of the wlad siyyed over the other villagers is in fact being questioned. This dimension of the legend can be read as a polemic ordering of symbols that makes a claim for legitimate domination, which in this case is symbolic domination. The legend does not claim special social or economic rights for the descendants of the saint but rather symbolic prerogatives, "specialness." This is what is today being contested by the non-wlad siyyed villagers.

THE LEGEND OF SIDI LAHCEN

Sidi Lahcen was the son of Sidi Masud, who was married to a woman from the Ait Bouhadou section of the Ait Yussi of Enjil tribe.

Sidi Lahcen left home at an early age, traveling first to el-Dila and then to Tamgrut. Arriving in Tamgrut, he found the master of the brotherhood, Sidi ben Nasr, lying critically ill, covered with sores oozing pus. His stench was so awful and his appearance so repulsive that the other students even refused to come to his bedside. Sidi Lahcen boldly approached the holy man and volunteered to wash his clothes. He brought the disease-ridden clothes to the river, where he not only washed them but drank the filthy rinse water. Sidi ben Nasr called his students to his bed and told them that he once had had great baraka, but now it had all passed to the Berber and there was none left for them.

When Sidi Lahcen decided to leave Tamgrut, Sidi ben Nasr said he would lead him out of the region on a mule. The local people were outraged to see a great saint leading a Berber. Ben Nasr replied to their taunts by saying that he was leading Sidi Lahcen's mule so that Sidi Lahcen would continue to look straight ahead. His baraka was now so powerful that the earth itself might follow him. At the edge of his territory (*bled*), Sidi ben Nasr gave Sidi Lahcen a gift and wished him well.

The Alawite sultan, Moulay Ismail, having heard that Sidi Lahcen was a great scholar, invited him to the capital. Upon arriving in Meknes, Sidi Lahcen found the sultan's workers building a fortified wall around the city. They were being pushed to the edge of exhaustion and pleaded with Sidi Lahcen to intercede on their behalf. That night at the palace, and each succeeding night, Sidi Lahcen smashed the dinner plates. The sultan was enraged. He sent for Sidi Lahcen and demanded an explanation. The saint told the sultan that he was only breaking clay dishes, whereas he, Moulay Ismail, was breaking the dishes of Allah (i.e., the workers).

In a fury, Moulay Ismail ordered Sidi Lahcen to leave his city. The saint agreed and pitched his tent in a cemetery at the edge of Meknes. Hearing this, Moulay Ismail rode to the cemetery and demanded to know why Sidi Lahcen had not obeyed his orders. Sidi Lahcen said he had. He had left the imperial city and was now in the city of Allah. If the cemetery was really within his realm, then the sultan should talk to his subjects, Sidi Lahcen taunted him. The sultan tried and failed. Sidi Lahcen called out, "s-salamu alaykom" (peace be with you) and the gravestones answered, "alaykom salam" (and peace be with you).

Humiliated, the sultan, his sword raised, charged Sidi Lahcen. Suddenly his arm froze above his head, and his horse began to sink into the ground. A wall of fire sprang up. Terrified, the sultan begged for his life, offering his kingdom to Sidi Lahcen. Sidi Lahcen refused the kingdom but told the sultan to have his scribe draft a decree freeing the shurfa. Decree in hand, Sidi Lahcen left Meknes.

He proceeded on to the Middle Atlas seeking a place to live. He stopped first near the village of Senhaja (an Arabic-speaking village some six kilometers from Sefrou). From the moment he pitched his tent there, the villagers pestered him to leave. He replied that he was *weld sharia,* literally "son of the Islamic law," that is, a learned and proper man, and that although he had the right to remain there he would leave. Sidi Lahcen's tent had been adjacent to a path leading to the village. Since the villagers had turned their heads when passing his tent, Sidi Lahcen cursed them by giving them crooked faces. To this day there is not a good-looking man in Senhaja.

Sidi Lahcen continued his search, camping next at the village of Azzaba (another Arabic speaking enclave in the region). Although the people of Azzaba were hospitable and wanted him to stay, Sidi Lahcen found the water disagreeable and left after several days.

Proceeding up a valley from Azzaba, he passed through the bled of an ascetic holy man who lived in a cave. This saint emerged as Sidi Lahcen was passing and sat and stared at him. He told some passing shepherds that a great saint was going to live among the *wlad abad,* the inhabitants of a nearby village. He said "I can see his halo (*norr*), stretching from the ground to the sky."

Just as Sidi Lahcen reached the hills which ring the village, his horse knelt down. At that time there was another saint in the village, Sidi Abderhaman. Sidi Lahcen asked the saint for hospitality and was granted it. The village and its bountiful, cold, running springs greatly pleased him. He decided to settle there. The wlad abad were happy to have him. They fed him and gave him land to farm and a woman to marry.

At that time intertribal warfare was raging in the region. The Ait Yussi tribe, upon hearing of the saint's arrival, implored Sidi Lahcen to settle in Tamzazit, the village of the wlad abad. The tribe held a great council, and each faction agreed to send one of its families to live in the village so that they would all have a common origin, *assal wahed*. They knew that Allah had sent them a great saint and that he was the pride, *horm*, of the tribe.

They wanted to hold a great celebration, *musem*, for him every year, but Sidi Lahcen said no; if it is too great, your children will abandon it. It is better to have a small one but one that will endure. There were soon two celebrations held every year, one for his birth and one for his death.

When Sidi Lahcen had first moved into the village, the wlad abad had come to him and offered him two bowls, one filled with milk and the other with water. He instructed them to mix the two liquids and then to separate the milk from the water. They tried and failed. From that point on, he told them, their descendants and his would be like the milk and water, inseparable. He cautioned the wlad abad that if his descendants were ever stupid—like a donkey—not to "ride" on them. Sidi Lahcen would take care of that.

Some time later, there was a fight involving one of the wlad abad and one of Sidi Lahcen's sons. Sidi Lahcen was greatly angered and cursed the wlad abad, killing them all but one. This man (as well as the families which came to the village later) are the ancestors of the present-day wlad abad. They made a contract stating that his descendants would be equal but that Sidi Lahcen would have the right to discipline (*rebbi*, to educate, chastise, raise) his descendants.

Shortly after the death of the saint, his son's wife entered his tomb and touched his cheek: there was still blood running in his veins. Sidi Lahcen struck her blind.

ANALYSIS OF THE LEGEND

The first section of the legend, which is brief but important, clearly states that Sidi Lahcen was born into a Berber family. This means that Sidi Lahcen was not born a sherif. Since his descendants do consider themselves shurfa, and in fact base their religious and social position on this identity, this paradox must be overcome.

To see how this is done, we must examine the concept of sherif-hood more closely. By definition, a sherif is a direct agnatic descendant of the Prophet Mohammed or, more precisely, of his son-in-law, Ali. Technically, therefore, it would be impossible for the original Berber inhabitants of Morocco to have been shurfa. There are, however, two large groupings of shurfa in Morocco: the so-called Drissin shurfa, who came to Morocco with Moulay Idriss at the end of the eighth century, and the Alawites. It should be emphasized that although both of these shurfa lines are prominent in Moroccan society, they are neither a caste, a class, nor even a corporate group. In addition to these two main lines of shurfa, there are hundreds, if not thousands, of other groups—usually descendants of saints—who claim to be shurfa. These groups have had their claims to divine grace validated by the local communities and their credentials as shurfa legitimated by the Alawite sultan. There are rich shurfa in Morocco and very poor ones, powerful and powerless, white and black; they share little more than the name. Just as the shurfa in Morocco are not a class, or even a group, they do not occupy any defined status position by virute of their being shurfa. Sherif-hood, in and of itself, does not carry any ascribed status. Rather, it is more likely to be an after-the-fact, symbolic legitimation of status achieved than itself the source of such achievement or position.

Given this general description, we must now examine how this concept of sherif-hood is viewed by the descendants of Sidi Lahcen themselves. They readily agree that everyone in the village is a Muslim. They maintain, however, that there is an essential difference between the shurfa and the non-shurfa or *awamm*, the "people." The wlad siyyed (shurfa) are superior to the non-shurfa. The reason for this is that they are "closer" to Allah, through the intermediary Sidi Lahcen, than are the non-wlad siyyed.

In what way are they "closer"? There is no commonly agreed-upon answer to this question. People simply say that the shurfa are "special," *xass*. This is sometimes associated with certain character traits. The shurfa are *mqelleq*, irritable, volatile, and capable of rash action. One can never be sure (they themselves do not know) when they might suddenly erupt into irrational action, perform a miracle or cure. Even if they are undistinguished from other people throughout their lives, there is always the possibility, the potentiality, of their performing extraordinary deeds or of their receiving divine assistance. Since they are "closer" to Allah, he might choose to communicate through them; this unpredictability and the volatility of their characters should be respected, even feared.

After an unproductive attempt on my part to draw out a further "theory of shurfa-ness," one of my informants told me the following story:

There were two friends, one a rich Berber and the other a poor Alawite sherif. The Berber lived in the countryside, and whenever he came to the city he stayed at the home of the sherif. One time the Berber and the sherif went to the mosque to pray. When the sherif bent over to begin his prayers, the Berber saw a bottle of liquor in his pocket. This upset him greatly but he was too embarrassed, *heshem*, to say anything about it. The two men returned to the sherif's house to sleep, but the Berber was so upset that he left in the middle of the night. He thought to himself "any man who brings whiskey to the mosque is no sherif." That night he had a dream: it was very, very hot and the sky was pressing almost to the ground. There were millions of people pushing and milling around in the brutal heat, the Berber was sweating and very thirsty. Ahead of him he saw a beautiful woman on a pedestal. She had a gold pitcher in one hand and a silver pitcher in the other. She was pouring cold water out of these into people's mouths as they filed past her. The Berber moved slowly closer toward the woman, but when he reached her she refused him the water, saying, "You have been bad to my children; what did you say to them yesterday?" The Berber woke up in a sweat and ran to the city to the sherif's house, woke him and begged his forgiveness. The sherif was happy to see his old friend again and when he heard why his friend had left in the middle of the night he forgave him and promised never to drink again. They became friends and the Berber told his friends to respect the shurfa no matter what they do, *andhum haqq bezzef.*

The key word here is *haqq.* The range of its meanings are listed in Mercier's dictionary: truth, right, justice, equity, legitimacy, obliged-ness. It is the possession of this quality, the "being" in this state, which make the shurfa special. What this really seems to be, therefore, is a doctrine of legitimate domination in Weber's sense. The shurfa are making a claim for the right to be set apart, to receive certain symbolic benefits, to be exempt from ordinary standards of judgment because (implicitly) they have this quality of "being" right, just, legitimate, in close connection with the divine.

This still leaves the problem of how this quality is transmitted. Several villagers maintained (when pushed by the anthropologist) that shurfa-ness was carried in the blood and therefore shurfa and non-shurfa should not marry as this would dilute the blood. Most villagers, however, refused to accept this version of the essence and mode of transmission of sherif-hood. The most common answer which villagers gave was that shurfa were shurfa and that is all there is to it.

The "specialness," the "right," really adheres in the symbols of sherif-hood and is transmitted through the symbols themselves. In any group of shurfa, only a few (if any) of the members of the collectivity are going to manifest this "specialness," this closeness to the divine. There is no way of knowing beforehand which individuals in the collectivity will actualize the potential; it depends on the personal character of the individuals involved.

The original source of the divine grace which is held to adhere in the group was personal charisma. The routinization of this power, however, was not fully or elaborately carried through on the social structural side. There has not been the creation of either a priesthood, or a hereditary caste, or a group of specialists, not even a fixed principle of succession. Rather, the routinization of charisma in Moroccan society (and this holds particularly for the wlad siyyed groups) was carried out on the symbolic level, by the articulation of a set of symbols which both formed and expressed a conception of divine power and how it appears in the world. What is passed along are these symbols which mark off and delimit a group (really a

collectivity because the groups share little but this common designation). Sherif-hood does not adhere in the blood; that was really the
wrong question. It adheres in the symbols surrounding the saint and in
the accepted designation of a group of men as descendants, protectors
of the saint's divine power. They protect and are guardians of the
symbols of holiness, and it is through these symbols that the holiness
is transmitted. The wlad siyyed are "closer," "special," "right,"
because they are the wlad siyyed.

The exception which proves the rule (and really articulates the
whole system) is the Alawites, who have succeeded in bringing the
symbols of legitimacy together with a new social role and a method for
continuous transmission of both. The primacy of the Alawite Sultanate in both the religious and political spheres has provided a
method for after-the-fact legitimation of new manifestations of
charisma. The sultan grants decrees to those saints who have already
had their personal charisma accepted on the local level, and this
increases and supports the legitimacy of both parties.

We thus have the basis for both a doctrine and a typology of
legitimate domination. The legend can be read as a gloss on this
doctrine. The religious master, ben Nasr, dominates his students on
the basis of his personal authority, his baraka. Were the students to
succeed in obtaining his baraka through the force of their own
powers, they would become masters. Sidi Lahcen not only deprived
the other students of the baraka of their master, he even threatened to
overshadow the master himself. Ben Nasr (with the appropriate
symbols of humiliation) had to lead Sidi Lahcen out of his territory.
Charismatic authority takes the form of courageous action and
personal presence; it commands its own submission.

In the incident concerning Sidi Lahcen's encounters with the sultan,
the theme of symbolic domination and submission becomes central.
Moulay Ismail was a great and powerful sultan in the process of
consolidating his kingdom and eliminating the various potential
antagonists who abounded in the countryside. He was cementing his
right to dominate; by obtaining submission from the saints he was
insuring his authority. By so doing, however, he was strengthening
their legitimacy, and that is why he was so successful. Sidi Lahcen was
indeed a great scholar and a holy man, but he was not a sherif. He
needed legitimation from the Alawite sherif. In the legend, Sidi Lahcen
carefully demarcates the realm in which he is willing to submit (the
political) and the realm in which Allah and not the sultan is sovereign
(the claim being that this realm is primary). There are the plates of
Allah and those of the sultan just as there is the realm of the sultan and

that of the saint. This is not to say that the sultan's political authority is being threatened, quite the contrary, but the limits of his legitimate domination are being drawn. It is an alliance for separation.

In the legend, therefore, the wlad siyyed are making a claim for the scope and depth of their own legitimacy. One should respect the wlad siyyed, exempt them from certain duties and standards of judgment, and not chastise them if they transgress certain bounds because they are "special," "volatile," "closer to Allah," and "andhum haqq bezzef."

These claims are explicitly developed in the legend in relation to the original inhabitants of the village. Sidi Lahcen tells them that his descendants are like milk and the others are like water. Although they should live side by side, in intimate contact and without social differentiation, he, Sidi Lahcen, will watch over his descendants. Milk is one of the symbols of the shurfa in Morocco, and the claims to symbolic domination are strong and clear. The wlad siyyed are the same as the other villagers except that they are protected (and chastised) by the saint; they are special. This is not a doctrine of social justice but a claim to legitimate domination in the symbolic realm. It is not a claim that the wlad siyyed should have special social and economic privileges. The wlad siyyed would be no more capable of separating the milk from the water than the original inhabitants. They are inseparable but not the same. Their legitimacy lies in the power of Sidi Lahcen, and their right is to symbolic prerogatives, particularly the acceptance of their "specialness." We will see that it is exactly this point which is today being contested by the non-wlad siyyed villagers.

The source of this charismatic authority and cornerstone of legitimacy in Morocco is *baraka:* the symbol which formulates and expresses the Moroccan conception of divine grace and supernatural power. Defined in the most abstract terms we could say something like "the manifestation of God's grace on earth." Baraka refers to divine grace or presence in whatever form it takes, and these forms are numerous (Westermarck gives examples for 225 pages).[2] Baraka can refer to people, states, substances, places, literally anything, and is essentially a cultural gloss on their qualities, a judgment of blessedness. Baraka is a good harvest or a good price for an animal. It is cool, clear, plentiful water; it is good health, business success, a good meal.

Rather than attempt a totalistic explanation of its place in Moroccan culture, I will instead narrow my focus to the place of baraka in the legend, where it appears in two distinct forms. In the second half of the legend, when Sidi Lahcen is searching for a special place in which to settle, an important consideration is the baraka of the place symbolized by water. Good, clear, cold, plentiful, running water is a necessity for the saint. It symbolizes the presence of God's grace, his bounty, at that particular place. Water is frequently used to express the baraka of a place but the availability of firewood, farmland, and game were also mentioned by the villagers. We have here a cultural comment on the worth of the place; it is filled with good things, and more will accrue to it. It is blessed by God. Otherwise why would it be so full of good things.

The first general point then is that baraka is a concrete quality of things in this world; God makes himself manifest through things. Further, baraka tends to breed and attract baraka: good water brings good crops, which brings a powerful saint, who brings supernatural aid and protection. The baraka of the land, its bounty, is complemented by the baraka of its saint, his holiness and power.

The main form that baraka takes in the legend, however, is as a quality of individual men, extraordinary men. Sidi ben Nasr is a master who possesses great erudition and practices exemplary piety. These qualities are both an expression of his baraka, his grace, his blessedness, as well as being the content of that grace and blessedness. When he is referred to as a man of great baraka, the reference is both to his personal qualities and to the form which divine grace takes on this earth.

This is highlighted in the encounter between ben Nasr and Sidi Lahcen. Sidi Lahcen, through a display of courageous and unquestioning loyalty and submission, is able physically to capture the baraka of ben Nasr. Transmission of baraka here takes place directly between two extraordinary men. Sidi Lahcen, through his force of character and his courage, shows himself to be a man of great baraka. He triumphs over his fellow students, who possessed a dogged loyalty but failed when their devotion was put to the test. They lost their chance of becoming men of baraka exactly because they "were" not men of baraka; they lacked the necessary qualities, they failed in the world. Sidi Lahcen, through absolute submission, achieved domination. He had arrived at Tamgrut as a student and he left as a saint.

Divine Grace shows itself through unusual sanctity, loyalty, submission, courage, force of character, strength, etc. Conversely, the appearance in the world of these qualities is symbolized as baraka. Through the symbol of baraka, divine grace, supernatural power is made concrete. Through this symbol the culture expresses its conception of the innumerable forms in which the divine appears in the world.

Baraka is its own legitimation. There is no way to predict its appearance or rationally to control or explain it. When it appears, one stands in awe of it, one fears and respects it. Divine power or presence can be a source of great bounty or equally a force which is terribly destructive for those not equipped to handle it. The woman in the last episode was blinded; the villagers who ignored Sidi Lahcen's dictates were killed. Hence the wlad siyyed, guardians of this symbol, should be given latitude because, potentially at least, they are likely mediums for the conveyance of baraka. They are special because they are more likely to possess baraka and to manifest it in the world; even if they behave like donkeys, one should not ride on them.

The final set of symbols which are central in the legend concern the nature of relationships, particularly those between a place, its inhabitants, and a saint. Saints in Morocco are often referred to as *mul bled*, literally "the master of the land," though the term means a great deal more than that.

Mercier's dictionary lists the following terms under bled: country, land, homeland, territory, property, domain, place, locality, region. Thus when one says of a saint that he is the master of the bled, the referrent is a complex one. The symbol bled is itself a term with deep and varied resonances, indicating a strong bond, a link, more than mere ownership or possession, although that too is often essential. If one gives a direct, static, unidimensional definition to such a symbol—the territory of, home of, administrative unity of, etc.—then the meaning is lost. The word emphasizes a more intense relationship of attachment, sympathy, a mutual partaking as well as a strong claim of domination and control. One says of an area that it is the bled of a particular saint. Either he is living there or he has perhaps performed a miracle on the spot, and this establishes a relationship between the saint and the physical locale. He will continue to watch over, protect, adhere to his bled. Ben Nasr had been the mul bled, but when Sidi Lahcen capured his baraka, ben Nasr had to undergo public humiliation (by leading the saint's donkey), lest the very land itself leave with Sidi Lahcen.

When these claims involve an element of possession, domination, or ownership, and, more particularly, when some sort of submission, obligation, or reward is entailed, there is often an element of contestation. Sidi Lahcen wins the right to settle in Tamzazit by outshining the saint who had been there before him, who willingly submits through his gesture of hospitality. Claims of domination and submission in Morocco are rarely so easily established, however, and usually must be reasserted, defended, remolded, and reinforced time and time again. There is a legend in the village of Senhaja (the village which had rejected Sidi Lahcen) of how the local saint, Sidi Yussef, and

Sidi Lahcen met in a sort of theological duel to decide who was to be the spiritual master of the Ait Yussi tribe. Sidi Lahcen won, and a special relationship was established between himself, his descendants, his tomb, and the Ait Yussi tribesmen.

Bled, then, is not simply a case of association, or a territorial designation, but it is a claim, an assertion of a more profound connection ("my country," "my turf"). It is a statement about a quality of relationship—an aggressive statement of a deep, emphatic, empathetic attachment of a mutual spiritual branding.

Mul is listed in Mercier as meaning: master, possessor, proprietor, patron, adherent, responsible, etc. Mercier then goes on to list some sixty examples of its use ranging from *mula-na*, our master, which refers primarily to Allah and secondarily to the sultan, through *mul-ferran*, keeper of the public oven. The term runs throughout all aspects of Moroccan culture and has strong overtones of domination and control. Just as the keeper of the public oven is responsible for its upkeep, regulation, and use, so all functions in Moroccan society through all its mediating levels up to Allah, who is the master, proprietor, and guardian of the universe, are owned, controlled, dominated, and not simply occupied. One is not merely the owner of a horse, a house, or intelligence; one is their master. So too with the saint's relations both to "his" bled and to the inhabitants of that bled. An intimate connection is established, and the connection is one of domination: mul bled, master of his domain.

The saint, by dint of his baraka, is master and lord of a domain, but—and this is another theme which runs throughout the legend and Moroccan society—he established his domination over the inhabitants of the bled contractually. Sidi Lahcen considers entering into this relationship with the villagers of Senhaja and Azzaba before proceeding to Tamzazit (later called Sidi Lahcen), where the process of negotiating his entry into the village and his establishment of relationships with the tribes in the region becomes the focus of the legend. He had negotiated with the sultan for his own legitimation, and he negotiates with the wlad abad for the legitimation of his descendants.

Moroccan social relations are explicitly cast in this contractual idiom. Mutual rights and obligations are spelled out publicly and in great detail for a wide range of relationships. The contract lasts as long as the parties maintain their obligations. If and when it disintegrates, it must be renegotiated. One encounters this in political affairs (elaborate series of pacts and alliances which form and reform), religious affairs (one contracts for a saint and with the saint for specific favors), economic affairs (business partnerships and agricultural pacts abound), and also social affairs (elaborate marriage contracts spell out exact rights, duties, and obligations of each party). It is a truly ubiquitous aspect of Moroccan social relations. The contractual basis of social relations is also their legitimation; one is obligated by the contract which one has negotiated because one has negotiated it. In this way Sidi Lahcen had negotiated with the original inhabitants of the village to be their mul bled and had stipulated certain conditions (not to "ride" on his descendants). When the contract is violated, he annihilates all but one of those villagers and then proceeds to renegotiate with the lone survivor.

The legend also emphasizes the contractual basis for the saint's relationship to the tribes. They come to him offering to submit to his spiritual protection. Each faction will move a family to the village if the saint will offer them a common spiritual ground, *assal wahed*. They then begin to negotiate the form that the celebration of the saint will take from that point forward. In the beginning was the negotiation.

Finally we can read the legend as a symbolic map of the region. In this version—and the polemic dimension is clear here—the wandering saint comes to the region in search of a spiritual home. There are really only three possibilities. These three are (today) the only Arabic-speaking enclaves in this Berber-speaking mountain area. Implicitly then the prime determinant of the cultural geography is language. The legend says that the saint, now also a sherif, would only settle in those villages which were Arabic-speaking. Along with language, two other criteria come into play. The first involves the people in the village and their character. The people in Senhaja are irascible and prone to controversy. According to their own legend, another saint, Sidi Yussef, who also camped next to their village, was also poorly treated and was planning to leave. But this time the villagers decided that they needed a saint and they forced him to stay against his will, beating him and tying him up. The villagers have never been able to sustain a *musem*, celebration, for their saint as they have been too factional and quite unable to cooperate. The baraka of their saint, Sidi Yussef, must have been weak, tired, thin (*ayyan*) to allow this to happen.

The people in Azzaba were friendlier, but their physical location— and this is the second main criterion—was inherently unworthy, as symbolized by their water. Senhaja had good water, so there was the possibility of baraka there. Azzaba has tepid, insufficient water, and hence it would have been inappropriate for a powerful saint to settle there. Azzaba eventually did have a saint come to it, an unlearned man who is often referred to mockingly by people in Sefrou and Sidi Lahcen. His celebration has also traditionally been small, if it is held at all. This is appropriate as his baraka was weak.

Sidi Lahcen, having been refused by the people of Senhaja and having himself refused Azzaba because of the lack of baraka in its physical setting, "naturally" came to settle in Tamzazit (today Sidi Lahcen). It had friendly people, eager to have the baraka of a great saint; it had its own baraka (cold and plentiful water); and negotiations were smoothly and effortlessly carried out.

The elements of the legend as a legitimating claim of domination are now complete. They range from the spiritual empathy between the saint, the earth itself, the inhabitants, the social and ecological possibilities of the region, the nature of divine grace, the form of its appearance and transmission in the world, to the historical conflict of the charismatic saints with the powerful centralizing forces of the Alawite Sultanate. We now can turn to the end of the nineteenth century and the beginning of the twentieth to examine the social, political, and religious position of the descendants of Sidi Lahcen at that time.

3. Dissidence and Mediation

Cultural Conceptions of Political Order in the Nineteenth Century

By the third quarter of the nineteenth century, the power and control of the sultan again began to be seriously and conspicuously undermined. Here, as in the seventeenth century, the weakening of the central government was coincident with (and partially engineered by) the increased European influence and strong internal reaction to the foreigners.

Political order, religious order, their interrelationships and separations, as well as the cultural conceptions of identity and holiness are the themes which reemerge. But this time they coalesce in quite a different form from the one we examined earlier, and offer a foil for the drastic changes which occurred after the entry of the French.

POLITICAL ORDER IN THE PRE-PROTECTORATE PERIOD

The distinction between *bled l-makhzen*—nominally defined as the land, domain, realm of the government or sultanate—and *bled s-siba*—conventionally called the realm of dissidence—has been one of the central concerns in histories of Morocco. In fact, however, things were never so neat, and the distinction needs recasting.

The standard definition of these terms, as developed by the French scholars and administrators in Morocco, states that bled l-makhzen and bled s-siba were opposed territories with separate and distinct governing institutions; one area was ruled by the central government, and the other was totally independent from the government, although recognizing the sultan as the leader of the Islamic community. The "realm of the government," according to this view, encompassed the plains and steppes of the country, and the realm of dissidence was found in the mountains. The plains and cities were thought of as being inhabited by Arabs and the mountains by Berbers, over whom the government had "no control."[1] Historically, this argument continues, Morocco was unified under the Almoravid dynasty in the twelfth century, but soon a split developed between the bled l-makhzen and the bled s-siba. The two areas developed separately from then on, "the *bled l-makhzen* gradually losing their Berber language to become Arabic speakers, operating under different social and political conditions and absorbing new cultural features. The *bled s-siba* remained the stronghold of mountaineers who retained their proud independence until the twentieth century, at which time the French subdued them."[2] The government-controlled territory was ruled by "Arab concepts of a centralized state with absolute political power theoretically concentrated in the hands of the ruler. Within this system the lines of command, of authority, and of control, were relatively direct and simple."[3] The Berbers were ruled by democratic councils of elders. Hoffman, summarizing the French sources, concludes his discussion of the problem with two charts, neatly juxtaposed, which illustrate and differentiate the supposed structure of the two realms.

This is a radically inadequate description. It is too spatial, too substantialist, and much too solid and corporate a view of Moroccan society. To outline a more acceptable version, though one which still lacks several vital dimensions, we turn to a summary of the *makhzen/ siba* split as described in 1903 by Aubin in his book *Le Maroc d'aujourd'hui.*[4]

What was the government? Simply enough it was the sultan, who since the seventeenth century had been a member of the Alawite dynasty, his court and ministers (plus their households), as well as an armed contingent of soldiers. In Aubin's day, the government kept as few as two thousand men under arms. These men were drawn from four large tribes, known as the *jaysh,* who had been resettled over a long period by the central government around the imperial cities of Fez, Marrakech, Meknes, and Rabat. They were, in effect, the only tribes directly and continuously under the sultan's command. It should be pointed out that there have been frequent uprisings even by these tribes who were, by definition, part of the government.

The touchstone, according to Aubin, for evaluating whether or not one was in bled l-makhzen or bled s-siba was threefold: (a) whether or not the tribes paid their taxes, (b) whether or not they supplied men for the sultan's expeditions, and (c) whether or not they would guarantee safe conduct through their territory for the sultan, his representatives, or his protectees. None of these was simply an either/or proposition but it was almost always a question of degree, of the relative strength at any given time of the actors involved. Some tribes could be made to meet all of the government's demands during a certain time, in some cases very lengthy periods, and others were sufficiently powerful to resist them for extended periods. All recognized the sultan as leader of the religious community. However, many found themselves in a more fluctuating position and would give as much as the government forced them to give, for as long as the government could maintain its superiority. These relationships would vary with the ascending and descending fortunes of the government and the various tribes. We are dealing here with a relationship between rural groups and the government, a shifting, constantly redefining interaction between groups over specific obligations — arms, money, men — and an equally important and concrete symbolic assertion and counterassertion — government realm versus realm of dissidence.

Before the French Protectorate, one of the basic institutional links between the tribes and the government was the *qaid*. Whenever its influence permitted, the government would appoint its own qaid-s in tribal areas. These qaid-s, however, were usually chosen from the powerful and influential men in that particular tribal section. Although occasionally the government was strong enough to appoint a complete outsider as qaid, more often it simply validated a local "big man." The shape and intensity of this relationship varied a great deal. Just as, in the broadest terms, the relative strengths of the central government and the tribes varied, altered, and shifted over time, so did the strength and importance of the position of qaid. The particular individual, whether appointed or approved, would be an extremely important variable in these relations. All of these dimensions resulted in a wide and extremely volatile range of relationships between the government, the tribes, and the qaid-s, and obviously precluded a rigid and static formulation.

The institutional importance of the qaid stems from his responsibility for collecting taxes, supplying soldiers, and insuring safe passage in his domain. In return for fulfilling these obligations, or some part of them, the government tacitly agreed not to interfere in his internal dealings with his fellow tribesmen. The government's demands — and this is the catch — were always high, usually higher than what the qaid could easily meet. Further, qaid-s powerful enough to meet them were not likely to be submissive to the government. These excessive demands or some portion of them were passed on from the qaid to his area of control; again, an explosive and renegotiable situation. The general principle for the government, of course, was to try to drain as much money and men as possible from the qaid and tribes—and to sustain symbolic domination—in order to increase its own wealth, power, and prestige. The idea was to impoverish the tribes so that they could not buy guns and horses, the basic ingredients of dissidence; "revolt follows prosperity."[5]

Counterresistance to this pressure was always present. When it reached the stage of successful defiance, then it became siba. Siba then is clearly not a concept that one could apply consistently to a certain territory, but was rather a state of dissidence within a common religious community. It was a dynamic, shifting, now receding, now advancing, see-saw parrying, with all parties concerned exerting varying pressures in more or less opposite directions.

Aubin, with my embellishments, has given us a clear account of the dynamics of dissidence. The main limitation of Aubin's description, however, is that it was written from the perspective of a viewer situated in Fez, the capital. Therefore I shift at this point from Aubin's general description of siba/makhzen to a more concrete narrative of the actors in the region of Sidi Lahcen in the early twentieth century. This concrete narrative will move us closer, sociologically, historically, and geographically, to the village itself and the wlad siyyed.

POLITICAL ACTIVITY IN THE REGION OF SIDI LAHCEN

From the end of the nineteenth century to the establishment of the French Protectorate in 1912, the central figures in our region were: the sultan (Moulay Abdel Aziz), two qaid-s (one in Sefrou and one in Zgan, a Berber village near Sidi Lahcen), the wlad siyyed, the "tribal" groups (Beni Warain, Beni Saddan, Ait Seghrouchen, Ait Helli, Ait Yussi), and, finally, the French whose entry brought the era to a close.

During the reign of the sultan Moulay Abdel Aziz (1895–1907) the entire region, beginning just outside—occasionally inside—the crenelated walls of Fez, continuing across the rich, wheat-growing Sais plain up to and through the walls of Sefrou, and beyond into the surrounding foothills of the Middle Atlas mountains, was in a state of turbulence.

At the opening of this period, the most powerful group, the one which was successfully raiding and looting the villages of the rolling Sais plain, as well as the area above Sefrou in the mountains, was the Beni Saddan. Other tribes in the region, or certain of their factions, joined together temporarily to make a successful, more or less collective effort to drive the intruding Beni Saddan out of the region.

Siba therefore, not only concerns the relations between the tribes and the central government but can also become an important intertribal and even intratribal matter. It is clear that during those periods of general and widespread turmoil, the government might cease to be one of the main political and military forces in an area. The arena would then be open for intertribal maneuvering and warring and possible action by the local qaid-s, trying to extend their power in the region. Such was the state in the region of Sidi Lahcen during this period. The momentarily united coalition of groups dissolved, once they had succeeded in driving the Beni Saddan intruders out of their region. Armed and mobilized, these groups now began to fight each other in typical Moroccan fashion. The Beni Warain faction gained an uneasy dominance and began to loot and pillage exactly in the manner of the Beni Saddan. Qaid Omar in Sefrou now found his walled oasis city separated from Fez. To remedy this situation, to restore the relative disequilibrium, he supplied the other competing factions in the region (especially the Ait Helli) with weapons.

The Ait Helli, whose center was Zgan, a Berber village near Sidi Lahcen, were led by a qaid who had been originally appointed by the sultan and hence was nominally submissive to him. With the help of the arms supplied by Omar in Sefrou— remember, he was rebelling against the government while supplying arms to a government qaid to fight another dissident group—the Ait Helli were able to rout the Beni Warain handily and wrest military control of the area, thus eliminating them temporarily as the main dissident group in the region and establishing themselves as the new major force of dissidence. The Ait Helli felt themselves so powerful and invulnerable that they pursued the fleeing Beni Warain into the sanctity of a saint's tomb, where they slaughtered them. Since the Beni Warain, in principle, should have been supernaturally protected there, the massacre was a great show of strength and arrogance.

The remnants of the Beni Warain, who had been the leading ravagers of the land between Sefrou and Fez before they were routed by the combined forces of the rural qaid in Zgan and the urban qaid in Sefrou, now sent a delegation to Fez to the sultan Moulay Abdel Aziz. They asked for rifles so they could join the government's fight against other dissidents in the north. The sultan granted their request and issued them guns, and they set off to fight on the side of the central government.

At this juncture, Omar, the qaid in Sefrou, was in an extremely powerful position. To counteract the rapid consolidations of Omar's power, the sultan found a member of the Ait Helli named Breybra, who had been in the royal jail in Marrakech. He released him from jail, and installed him as the qaid in Zgan, while providing him with the necessary arms to counterbalance Omar. With the help of these arms, Breybra quickly mobilized his forces in the mountains.

Because of this, the sultan also supplied arms to Omar. With this aid, Omar managed to bribe one of Breybra's brothers into betraying him. Breybra, finding his own family feuding, was forced to retreat and never succeeded in reestablishing his alliances. His power disintegrated with amazing rapidity, and he was forced to flee for his life. He fled from Zgan with his family, leaving four wives in Sidi Lahcen, where they were granted the sanctuary of the saint. Breybra himself fled to the territory of the Beni Saddan and there asked for asylum from the sultan who granted him his life.

In the meantime, Qaid Omar in Sefrou had sent soldiers to Sidi Lahcen to demand that the wives and children of Breybra be surrendered to him. The descendants of the saint refused and sent a delegation to the sultan in Fez to demand that he make Omar respect the sanctuary of the saint. The sultan agreed and Omar's troops withdrew.

This intertribal strife, which was so widespread throughout Morocco, suddenly became an anachronism when the new sultan, Moulay Hafid, who himself had come to office on a xenophobic, anti-Christian wave, was forced to call in the French to protect himself. The military entry of the French signaled the end of an era in Moroccan history.

Political order in pre-Protectorate Morocco was anything but simple, substantial, and stable. All the antagonistic factions recognized the sultan as the leader of the Islamic community; symbolic recognition of his religious role had been stabilized. Submission to his political and financial claims was quite another matter. The word "claim" is the central one here. Bled l-makhzen is that area, group, faction, or individual who had accepted the sultan's claims to political and financial obligations. To put it more accurately, it was the realm where the sultan could enforce these claims. Bled s-siba—it should be recalled that the term "bled" itself implies a claim—was the realm of dissidence, both symbolic and financial. It was really a counterclaim, an assertion of power and independence.

Political loyalties in Morocco were (and are) attached to specific actors, and not to roles or institutions per se. A powerful sultan, who could make his claims stick, commanded loyalty as long as he was powerful. The roller-coaster careers of the qaid-s are an excellent example of this. Breybra was leading the tribes and threatening the sultan one week and fleeing for his life the next, with his cohorts and kin expressing no residual loyalties. He was the sultan's qaid only when the sultan could dominate him. In Morocco, political loyalty correlates only with the wielding of political power.

When the sultan achieved his claims to domination, it was usually because he had adroitly balanced competing factions in a region, countered or eliminated possible loci of dissidence, or united the competing factions against external opponents. Power (symbolic, military, economic, and personal), not force alone, was the name of the game. The system did have several articulation points—the sultan and the qaid-s. Their importance, however, depended on their personal presence. The shapes these struggles took over the past three hundred years followed no simple pattern. Variability, flux, redefinition, and on-going testing of wills were the rule.

Although the particular, concrete form varied enormously from period to period, from sultan to sultan, from area to area, the basic symbolic formulations of political order—bled l-makhzen and bled s-siba—provided the continuity from the time of the Alawites through the arrival of the French.

SOCIAL ACTION AND SOCIAL IDENTITY

One other concept, which has not yet been discussed, has been the source of much confusion. *Qbila* is usually translated as "tribe," but this proves to be a highly misleading translation. Qbila really indicates a culturally specific category which can be used to make a claim to common social identity. This commonality itself may have a variety of sources, and it can refer to groupings as small as the household or as large as the nation. If we understand it as a group's way of claiming social identity with no necessary, fixed social structural referent, then such famous questions as "Qu'est-ce qu'une 'tribu' nord-africaine?" are poorly posed. There are no "tribus" in Morocco, there are qbila-s.

By examining the basis of the qbila-s in the region of Sidi Lahcen we shall be able to understand the place and importance of the wlad siyyed. We have previously spoken of various groups who share a common name—Ait Yussi, Beni Warain, etc. These are often referred to as qbila-s. They are not clearly defined territorial units. Within the immediate area of Sidi Lahcen there were several groups who identified themselves with different named qbila-s (for example, Ait Yussi,

Ait Helli). Thus, if in broad terms the area around Sidi Lahcen was referred to as "Bled Ait Yussi," this does not mean that only groups identifying themselves as Ait Yussi lived within the territory. Bled, like qbila, implies a thing claimed but one which is highly localized; having a group of Ait Yussi living next to a group who identify themselves as Ait Helli is no contradiction. The groups in a region may make a claim to the same identity, but the claims made and their implications are not primarily territorial. This also varies according to context. Thus, if a man from another region of Morocco asked someone the name of his qbila, the respondent, even if he were from the wlad siyyed, might identify himself as "Ait Yussi." He would never give this answer in his village. Territory is a dimension of identity claims but it is not its source.

The qbila of the Ait Yussi as a whole has no overarching (or latent) social structural organization binding the various localized groups who share the common name together, either socially or politically. There is no fictive genealogical connection between the localized groups. There is one major distinction which the Ait Yussi make; there are the Ait Yussi of the plain—those groups living in the area between Fez and Sefrou—and the Ait Yussi of the mountain—those living in the foothills of the Middle Atlas in the vicinity of Sidi Lahcen. The split is based on ecological criteria; that is, the crops ripen sooner in the lowlands. This is important for organizing the festival for Sidi Lahcen but seems to have no other consequences. Each of the two regional divisions has an unequal number of local settlements (again, place rather than kinship is the relevant variable) and their only common activity is the saint's festival. As they say in the legend, it was the saint who gave them a common origin, *assal wahed,* and it is only in honor of the saint that they undertake any common activity.

What the Ait Yussi share, therefore, is a common name and a common saint. It should be added that not all qbila-s have a common saint. For the Ait Yussi the saint is particularly important to share because he affords them a common origin, *assal,* and thus secures their identity. Origin is an absolutely fundamental dimension of cultural identity in Morocco. The worst tragedy for a group or individual is to have an unknown origin. We shall see that one of the charges leveled by the wlad siyyed against the wlad abad in the village, and which has been the most difficult to answer, is that they do not know their origin. They have a common name but no common origin, and this is disgraceful.

Thus the referent of the qbila Ait Yussi is a double one; it refers first to the localized groups who identify themselves as Ait Yussi; this is really a claim of attachment to the locale and/or collectivity. Secondly, it refers to the various localized groups who come together to celebrate the saint, share in his baraka, and affirm their assal.

The qbila of the wlad siyyed is formed on a slightly different basis from that of the Berbers. The wlad Sidi Lahcen share a common name as well as a common origin. But, in addition, they have a common genealogy connecting them to the saint. They also speak Arabic. These two "facts" differentiate them as a qbila from the surrounding Berbers. When the wlad siyyed refer to the Ait Yussi, they do not differentiate themselves as "saints" as opposed to "tribesmen" but rather as "Arabs" as opposed to "Berbers." Everyone in Sidi Lahcen speaks Moroccan Arabic. Despite the fact that they live in the midst of so-called Berbers and that the importance of the village has stemmed from their role as mediators, many of the villagers do not speak Berber although most of them probably understand it to a degree. There are two reasons for this. Simply enough, all the Berber men speak Moroccan Arabic, and thus there is no "need" for the villagers to speak Berber. This puts them in a dominant postion vis-à-vis the Berbers, who must speak to the villagers in what to them is a second language. The language factor is played upon and the accents and mistakes of mountain people are mocked by the villagers (much as the people in Sefrou mock the villagers' accent). There is a more important reason why so few villagers know or will admit to knowing Berber. Arabic, and particularly the self-identification as an Arabic speaker, is an important aspect of the villagers' identity as descendants of the saint, as religious adepts, and as a culturally dominant group. Every one of the saint's descendants was adamant that he was an Arabic speaker and very few would readily admit that they spoke or even understood Berber. Thus, as all the Berbers speak Arabic, an important dimension of identity for the villagers became self-consciously not knowing Berber. Language, name and origin formed the basis of their cultural and social identity claims.

MEDIATION AND ITS CULTURAL BASIS

The basic social institution which stemmed from this difference in cultural identity and which linked the Berber groups and the wlad siyyed was mediation. If two groups in a Berber village were having a dispute which they could not resolve, they might decide to have the wlad siyyed mediate it. If so, they would come to the village bearing various gifts of animals or money and offer them to the saint. Having made their offering, they would then approach those of the wlad siyyed who were known as the mediators that could best help them. If the wlad siyyed agreed, they would go to the disputants' village. Upon arriving, the party of mediators would proceed directly to the local mosque, often only a small mud building, or a tent, little different in appearance from the other buildings in the village. There they would wait and chant the Koran while their arrival was being announced. It was thus made a public affair and signaled the disputants' agreement to have the affair mediated and to abide by the decision. Shortly thereafter, the parties to the dispute would come to the mosque bearing presents of animals, food, money, and clothes. They were expected to feed their guests, lavishly and generously, for the duration of the mediation. Accepting mediation was an expensive affair.

The wlad siyyed mediators would first summon old men from the village and question them on the nature and specifics of the conflict. They always chose old men first because they were religious, that is, they were afraid (*ka-y-khof-u-men*) of Sidi Lahcen and Allah and so would be more likely to tell the truth. The wlad siyyed would present their decision publicly to the parties concerned and whoever else wanted to hear and then leave the village. The decision was *b-s-sif*, literally "by the sword," that is, it was definitive and without appeal. One refused to accept it or transgress its terms under threat of retribution from Sidi Lahcen—a powerful deterrent, but one that frequently proved insufficient.

During the time of siba, the immediate pre-Protectorate period, villagers recalled several cases of murder. Here the mediators would have to decide on the amount of the blood money, *diya*, to be paid to the offended family. Blood feuds, which seem to play a central part in the popular image of the "Arab," were rather infrequent in this part of Morocco, and when they did occur they were usually quickly adjudicated. More common types of disputes that called for mediation included boundary problems, quarrels over ownership, irrigation rights, stolen animals, etc.

The word is used—appropriately—to describe these mediation activities is *sellah*, which means to fix, patch up, or repair. One of the primary functions of the mediators was to serve as neutral and respected intermediaries who "patched up" disputes in which both parties wanted a solution but in which neither wanted to appear as having conceded. The patched-up quarrels were often reopened after a lapse, and the mediators were brought in again for repair work. The image of a temporary, patchwork settlement is thus more apt than one of binding arbitration.

Ironically, the last significant emergence of arbitration was in the context of the establishment of the French Protectorate. While the French were in the process of organizing their military control of the region during the period 1912–25, they encountered armed resistance from the Berber tribesmen. The French were eager to ease the transition to their rule, especially in such symbolically important matters as the surrender of arms. The Moqaddem Hamid—literally "the one who stands in front," "our leader"—acted as a new kind of middleman. The Berbers would come down from their mountain hideouts and deposit their arms with him; he would then inform the French, who agreed not to take further reprisals. This proved to be a particularly satisfying solution for the Berbers, who thereby avoided the sacrifice of their dignity by having to surrender to the Christians.

In the early years of the Protectorate the old system of mediation continued to retain its judicial importance, and the Moqaddem Hamid continued his active role, especially since the tribesmen were reluctant, to say the least, to deal with the French. For a short period he acted as a sort of judge for the whole region. As a transitional arrangement, the French were satisfied with this system, although they were not to sustain it for long. The mediatory agency of the wlad siyyed nearly ceased during the Protectorate.

THE MOQADDEM HAMID: A MAN OF BARAKA

In each of the historical periods, certain men epitomized the values, beliefs, and practices central to village life at that time. Such a man was the Moqaddem Hamid. He is unique in our chronicle for there was a shared consensus among the individuals and groups in the village both on values and his positive exemplification of those values. Because this harmony was so unusual, he rapidly became a legend. And so, during the last seventy years, few substantive details about him have passed down in the village.

One of the advantages, for the ethnographer at least, of the high level of discord and mutual antagonism which this society has raised to the level of life style, is that what admirers of a particular figure will not tell you, opponents often will. Whereas historical exactness is usually not found in either version, the intersection of the portrayals often yields a locus of the value upon which the disputes centered. Disharmony, which is the rule for all the other key figures we will examine, produces a more elaborate cultural and historical portrait.

In those rare cases of accord, what we lose in specificity of detail or richness of social reference is made up for in the affirmation of agreed-upon value through this process of legend making and deliberate obliteration of contrary detail. The primacy of the central cultural symbols, which in Morocco tend to be strongly drawn in absolute terms, comes to the fore when harmony exists between central actors, community values, and competing groups and individuals. Absent here are the undercutting, modifying, and outright contradiction brought about through the interplay of the clearly demarcated symbols and the complex social web of interaction and conflict. The following tale is highlighted by its equanimity.

The Moqaddem Hamid belonged to one of the lineages which claim descent from Sidi Lahcen Lyussi, the wlad siyyed. The phrase that was most often used to characterize him was that he was a *rajel baraka*, a man blessed by Allah. The legend of the Moqaddem Hamid stresses the fact that he was not only a member of the wlad siyyed, but was directly endorsed by the saint himself. Although all the descendants of a saint are considered potential possessors of his spiritual power and blessedness, it is usually only one or a few of them who are seen as the real inheritors of his power. The story goes that one day, commanded by a dream, he went to the tomb of the saint and, opening it, found a white *tarbouch* (turban). This was taken to be the tarbouch of Sidi Lahcen himself and striking confirmation of the baraka of the Moqaddem Hamid. The turban is thus the sign of connection to the saint. It is also a cultural symbol of the continuity and physical embodiment of holiness, of its literal transmission, as with the saint himself. The difference in the mode of transmission and the level of courage necessary to effect the transfer also indicate the evaluation of the degree of holiness involved, significantly less for the Moqaddem Hamid than for Sidi Lahcen.

What was the nature of blessedness at this time? What was the cultural conception of the just and holy man during this period?

The two main themes which dominate the image that has been formed of the Moqaddem Hamid are those of generosity and fairness. Because of his generosity, people said he was like the father of the whole Ait Yussi tribe and of everyone in the village. His door was never shut and anyone, sherif or non-sherif, known or unknown, was welcome at the house of the Moqaddem Hamid. Throughout the entire region and even beyond, people (and the word used here is *nas*, a general term not differentiating between "Berbers," "Arabs," etc.) knew that they could always come to his house and find tea or a meal, even if he had no advance warning; he was a true rajel baraka. The Moqaddem Hamid helped everyone: travelers who were passing through the region, students studying in the mosque, and poor families suffering through a difficult time.

The image of goodness and holiness was equated with that of generosity and even-handedness. This was not a time of ecstatic possession, astounding miracles, or even urbane scholarliness, but one of simple and direct piety. The image itself is a key one both in its outlines and in its modesty. It was universally agreed that the open generosity practiced by the Moqaddem indicated his blessedness—a strong comment on the community's values and the difficulty of living up to them.

As his fame spread and as he did more favors for people, they (*nas*) would spontaneously go out of their way to assist him. Again, this is rather untypical behavior. The Moqaddem himself did no manual labor; other villagers or men from the region made sure his trees were cared for and his fields plowed. He had no enemies and belonged to no factions. He was the true sherif.

The story of the Moqaddem Hamid is a very clear symbolization of the Moroccan conception of the virtues of piety, and the connection between religion and its rewards. The true sherif is one who is generous, and from his generosity bounty accrues to him. The good man belongs to no faction and favors no group. This trait of the Moqaddem is considered even more amazing than his generosity, and its rewards are immediate, material, and continuous. He who receives all equally will receive from all. Generosity and fairness breed wealth and spiritual power; spiritual power in turn breeds generosity and fairness, and so the cycle continues. The strength of the image, the clarity of its portrayal, and the clearness of the sentiments are all the more indicative of the difficulty and infrequency of its occurrence.

The Moqaddem Hamid was the last man in Sidi Lahcen to possess such qualities, to be perceived as a rajel baraka. Others since then have had supernatural powers, various virtues, or have achieved powerful positions, but none has been a rajel baraka. The era has changed, the position of the villagers has deteriorated, and their social role has been undercut; but the nature of the symbolism of the good man has changed much more slowly. The unanimous statements of praise for the Moqaddem Hamid are tinged with pathos for an era which has gone; they are always used as an uncomplimentary reflection on the present age.

4. The French Protectorate

Impact and Reactions

During the siba period, the possession of land was not the primary source or expression of wealth, power, or prestige. Disparities in land holdings do not seem to have been significant, at least in the villagers' view of their past. The outstanding exception to this rule was the Moqaddem Hamid, who is said to have owned an extensive amount of land. However, much of the produce from his land was redistributed.

The village served as a religious center for the warring tribes; it was *horm*, sanctuary, a somewhat calm island in a turbulent region. Because of this configuration the village also attained a certain economic importance. The *suq*-s, or markets, in the region, which today are crucial centers of commerce, played a considerably smaller role during the time of siba. The general reason for this was the insecurity which prevailed both in the region as a whole and within the markets themselves, often the scenes of violence. As the wlad siyyed were afforded a degree of immunity because of their religious prestige, they traveled to the suq-s, bought goods, and sold them in their stores in the village. Next to the Moqaddem Hamid, the two wealthiest men in the village were both storekeepers. As there was little money in circulation, the Berbers would barter (mostly grain and animal produce) for their purchases (tea, oil, sugar, rifles, and cartridges). The input of grain was a factor in minimizing the need for agricultural activity during the period.

With the establishment of the French Protectorate in 1912—an event remembered with a poignant ambivalence (positively because it ended the fear and insecurity of the siba period, and negatively because the Christians were now ruling a Muslim land)—the very nature of the region, its foci, values, and orientations were to alter drastically. A series of changes instituted shortly after the establishment of the Protectorate, and the villagers' reactions to these changes, were to have profound implications. Once the French were in control, the villagers felt themselves to be "reacting" to events, institutions, and values coming to them from the outside.

One of the first changes that the French made was to set up five markets in the Sefrou region as well as to shore up the older ones. Physical security, markets bolstered by the French, large inputs of foreign goods, and new needs all combined to undercut the economic role of the stores in Sidi Lahcen. Today there are nine stores in the village, and none produces sufficient revenue by itself to support a single family.

The next set of changes which the French instituted had an even more fundamental effect on village life. The French pursued a general policy of minimizing transhumance (for security reasons) and of "rationalizing" agricultural practices. They reactivated an agricultural tax, the *tertib*. The tax had first been introduced as a part of a European-directed fiscal reform under the sultan Moulay Abdel Aziz but, owing to the weak government during the siba period, had never been collected. The French collected it, thus initiating a basic reworking of the dynamics of the region. The overwhelming force of the French enabled them to introduce and enforce a series of similar reforms which had previously been unthinkable. There was very little the villagers could do against such measures except complain and submit. Even the smallest land holding was taxed under the tertib, and everyone had to pay something; this symbolic submission, more than the money itself, created an enormous reservoir of resentment against the French. The wlad siyyed in particular were humiliated because one of their essential rights which they had enjoyed as shurfa was exemption from the standard taxes. Having to pay taxes was a symbolic pronouncement to them of the coming deterioration of their status.

In order to carry out the tax program the French had to survey the land holdings. They sent teams from the city to carry out the survey, which opened the door to tremendous abuse. It was, indeed, the shift from the pre-Protectorate system of local justice (in which the wlad siyyed played such a key role) to the Protectorate system (in which the courts and the cities were to be given disproportionate power) that undid the general position of the wlad siyyed.

Shortly after the First World War, the French administration decided to build a school for the training of Moroccan military officers. They chose the village of Sidi Lahcen, both because of its excellent water supply and because it was already a focal point in the region. A delegation was sent to the village to propose building the school as well as a new road connecting Sefrou to Sidi Lahcen.

The village elders, the Moqaddem Hamid, and one of his brothers, the fqi Omar, also a highly respected religious teacher, vigorously opposed the idea and prevailed upon the other villagers to reject the proposal. The Moqaddem feared that if the school and road were built, the young men of the village would be lured away from their Koranic studies and turned into Christians. The villagers unanimously agreed to reject the offer. The French accepted their decision and built the school instead at Ahermoumou, a Berber village, some forty kilometers away.

The decision turned out to be crucial for the future of the village and was instrumental in shaping its fate for the next forty years. Although the Moqaddem Hamid thought he was guaranteeing that the village would remain a religious center, what he was actually guaranteeing was that the villagers would become farmers. By setting an anti-French and anti-modernist tone, the decision paradoxically pushed the villagers toward a role in which those religious values stood little chance of enduring. The French, following a policy of not forcing particular institutions where there was strong local antagonism to them, made no further proposals. The young villagers today unanimously condemn the Moqaddem's decision.

Before the establishment of the French Protectorate in 1912, the villagers did not conceive of themselves as farmers. Their primary self-conception was either as wlad siyyed mediators or rural countrymen, *bedawiyen*, but not farmers, *fellaha*. Even today, when agriculture has become increasingly central to the activities of the village, they see their olive growing as more important then their farming. During siba the amount of land under cultivation was limited by the general conditions of insecurity which prevailed, by the smaller population and its lower density, and by the alternative sources of subsistence (game and flocks). The new conditions brought about by the entry of the French caused a basic change in the cultural ecology of the whole region; agriculture became the dominant form of economic activity.

It is important to emphasize again that even today the villagers refuse the identity of farmer: pastoralist or saint, yes; peasant, no. They are not deeply rooted in their farmland, either by any "mystical ties to the soil" or by any important symbolic elaboration of identity.

Agricultural expansion and pressure for land were to become central during the period following the imposition of the French Protectorate. To understand the implications of these changes for village life, it is necessary to show the form which the expansion took. The choices were limited. The agricultural land which lies between the hills encircling the bowl-like valley of Sidi Lahcen totals roughly three hundred hectares. Today approximately two hundred and fifty of them are under cultivation, a significantly higher percentage than in the pre-French period. I will refer to this area within the valley as the "core" land area.

At the beginning of the French Protectorate the center of the village was at the back of this valley, nestling against one of the hillsides. Each of the hills which form the rim of the valley was, and is, not only a natural boundary to the "core" area but a social one as well. The first set of hills, behind the mosque and saint's tomb, marked both the limits of *horm* of the saint and the outer limits of the agricultural land of another of the village clusters. Because of this, expansion to the north was impossible. Directly to the south of the core area lay another set of hills. Behind these hills the land was owned jointly by several factions of the Ait Yussi who used the land for agriculture and grazing; expansion southward was thus blocked.

The mountainous land to the west of the core area was extremely sandy and covered with dense scrub. Even if it had been cleared, the soil was so poor and erosion so severe that it would not have been productive. Agricultural expansion could therefore occur only toward the east. Extending some five kilometers beyond the edge of the core area over a series of lightly forested, rolling hills, this land was bounded by a large river. Before the siba period it had been grazing ground for the transhumants' herds. During the height of siba, however, the intensity of grazing had diminished, turning it into a no-man's-land.

The French, who instituted and vigorously pursued a policy of encouraging sedentary agriculturalists, and discouraging trans-humants, surveyed the area shortly after the imposition of the Protectorate. They offered the rights to anyone who would clear the land of scrub and put it under cultivation. It should be stressed that before the Protectorate large areas of land in this region were not being exploited. Low population density and the general insecurity of siba combined to leave large stretches of land idle much of the year.

The net result of the French policies—new land under cultivation, the ending of siba, and the undercutting of the traditional functions of the wlad siyyed—was a drastic shift in the whole form of socio-economic activity in the village. Agricultural expansion and economic consolidation became the new basis of power within the village. Over a period of twenty-five years the amount of land cultivated doubled. This dramatic transposition is easy to grasp in a concrete manner since the land added was separate from but adjacent to the core area.

The core area includes some 245 acres of cultivated land, 70 percent of which is irrigated—an extremely high figure for this part of Morocco. Given the irregularity of the rainfall in the region and the precarious economic margins on which most villagers operate, irrigation offers a very important guarantee of crops. The crude agricultural techniques result in very low productivity with or without irrigation. However, irrigation does provide a safeguard against total failure.

The "secondary" area, while stretching over a much broader territory, accounts for some 230 hectares of cultivated fields. This rocky, rolling countryside is inferior in quality to that of the core area. The land has been covered with forest and scrub and even today has only been partially cleared. Only about 20 percent of the secondary land is irrigated, as opposed to 70 percent of the core land. Even the springs in the secondary area are not as reliable as those in the core area, and drainage is a severe problem.

Nonetheless, expansion into the secondary area has been of vital importance for the village. The population has grown at a very high rate over the last seventy years, and additional sources of food and income have become essential. There has been a marked change from a situation in which everyone had sufficient food and farmland was not a prime commodity, to one in which large differentials in land holdings, income, and olive trees exist.

One of the factors instrumental in altering the basis of village activity was the French support of the lawcourts. As we have seen, the village's importance stemmed from the complex of religious institutions; the village was a sanctuary, its inhabitants were mediators, it contained the baraka of Sidi Lahcen. The French pacification of the countryside reduced to insignificance the importance of the sanctuary. The role of mediators was eroded by the rise of the lawcourts as the primary institution for handling disputes. The office of *qadi*, religious judge, was not a French invention (as the secular courts were) but it had never had a significant role in this rural setting. There had always been strong resistance to the central government and generally to any nonregional interference. What the French did, in the name of preserving indigenous institutions, was to give the court system a centrality and force which it had never had before. By reinforcing and shoring up the courts, they undermined the mediation function of the wlad siyyed, thus contributing to a breakdown of the regional focus. The villagers understood what was happening, and several seized on the new base of power. By attaching themselves to the French-supported courts, they put themselves in an unassailable position.

As one insightful old man put it, the French brought security to Morocco not so much with their army as with their judges and jails. They not only brought security, they also brought a significant degree of centralization and control. The French-supported courts were both more powerful and less legitimate than the mediation of the wlad siyyed. It is exactly for this dual reason that they had such a major effect on the region and the village. The legitimacy of the wlad siyyed inhered in the fact that the disputing parties came to them for arbitration. The wlad siyyed were a means by which the tribes could publicly settle disputes they wanted to settle; the very function of the wlad siyyed in mediation was to legitimate. They were not initiators of the proceedings and had no form of worldly sanction if their decisions were not respected.

The French-backed courts, to the contrary, owed their appeal to the fact that they were powerful and not particularly legitimate. The French looked upon power as one of their main virtues. The Moroccans saw it as a new and potent source of manipulation without the threat of supernatural retaliation. The fact that they were powerful was to have dire consequences for many villagers; two village men became religious judges and used the courts and the French support of them to their own advantage. Aside from these dramatic instances, however, the power of the courts was brought into play in many other situations. Litigation was rapidly included in the repertoire of strategies which were employed to further one's position and assert one's dominance. If one could successfully win a court case, one had, for the moment, the power of the French on one's side. Because of this the courts became a prime locus of dispute.

The sanctions at the court's disposal were fines and jail, neither of which, in the long run, proved very effective in Morocco. Jail carried no social stigma. Men would willingly go to jail rather than pay fines (they were given the choice) and then reopen the dispute which had led to the litigation in the first place. There was little if any finality attached to the court's decisions; for this very reason they were rapidly accepted. Defying the courts was seen as manly assertiveness and as a personal matter without communal or supernatural overtones. In mediation, on the other hand, blatant disregard of a decision meant public flouting of the saint's power and of the legitimacy of the community; it happened frequently, but it was a different sort of act. Defying the wlad siyyed was *hashuma*, inappropriate and shameful; defying the courts was an indication of manly strength, *shih*.

With the rise of the courts, "justice" became more of an individual and less of a community affair. With the removal of the judicial process to Sefrou, the regional focus diminished as other villagers no longer witnessed the public mediation. Connections and understanding of the courts' processes became crucial, and legitimacy was no longer centered in the regional matrix. Consequently, if one had sufficient force, wealth, or influence, one could do as one liked. In the time of siba, people would say: "If you do not *heshem* (if you are not embarrassed), you can do as you please." The controls were those of the community and sheer force. This expression changed during the Protectorate to: "If you do not have money, your words are bitter" (*ila m'andek l'flus, klamek messus*). The tone changed from one where moralistic considerations were central to one where force, influence, and connections (now symbolized by money) were the prime considerations. This is not to say that force, money, influence, assertive character, or dynamism had not been central dimensions of the arena before, but only that one of the very few intermediate-range institutions which existed to limit, cajole, and temper this force had been annulled. One institution had been replaced by another, but by that replacement a whole set of variables which had come together to make the region the focus of social and cultural life in Morocco were now undermined and recombined in a new form. By bolstering the courts, the French took matters out of the local matrix in which they had operated and in which many other dimensions—economic, social, and political—had interplayed, forming a rather imperfect union but a union nonetheless. By sapping the legitimacy of the institutions, the French themselves created a sociocultural siba.

VILLAGE GROUPS AND STRATEGIES

Within this new sociocultural context, village groups and individuals reacted in widely divergent fashions. Again, the basic political parameters had been set from the outside. One group and several individuals understood rather rapidly some of the implications of the change. Although they succeeded, through various strategies, in achieving and consolidating social and economic position, none of them managed to foresee and understand the cultural implications both of the entry of the French and of their own reactions to it.

Each of the four wlad siyyed lineages of Sidi Lahcen trace their origins back to one of the four sons of Sidi Lahcen. Most of the descendants of two of the sons—Sidi Mohammed and Sidi Hamid—live in Roda; the others are divided among the other three parts of the cluster. Roda, the site of the saint's tomb, is by far the largest of the settlements, containing over half of the total population (roughly 900) and practically all of the non-wlad siyyed.

Until the siba period the Sidi Mohammed lineage was more powerful and influential than the Sidi Hamid. Its members were guardians of the saint's baraka and more prosperous than men of the other lineages. They were "closest" to the saint, in the double sense that their houses clustered around the tomb and that the men from this group supervised the mosque.

At the beginning of the siba period, however, several events signaled a rapid collapse of their collective fortunes. The sons of a man of the Ait Sidi Mohammed sublineage were unable to reach agreement on the division of their inheritance. The source of contention was several books purportedly written by Sidi Lahcen himself and therefore a source of great baraka. Unable to reach an equitable solution, the disputants decided to divide the books literally by ripping each in quarters. This act, the story goes, so outraged Sidi Lahcen that he devastated them, scattering them from his sanctuary by suddenly involving them in a series of violent incidents. Two Ait Sidi Mohammed sublineages became embroiled in a series of disputes culminating in a murder (the first of several which marked the period) between sons of parallel cousins. The weaker sublineage was forced out of the village; they settled twenty kilometers away in a section of the Ait Yussi which offered them land and hospitality. A third sublineage was also involved in this spate of violence, and they too were forced to flee the village.

Today the dominant lineage of the wlad siyyed is the Ait Sidi Hamid. It is composed of four sublineages of unequal size and importance. Two of these will not be discussed in detail because of their numerical insignificance and because they form "average" groupings in the village; their land, olive, and irrigation holdings are in direct proportion to their numerical size. Further, they have produced no particularly important individuals in the last fifty years, nor have they succeeded in acting as a group.

The two main sublineages are the Ait Ghazi ben Allal and Ait ben Shedli. The Ait Ghazi ben Allal is the sublineage to which the Moqaddem Hamid and his brothers belonged and the one which rose to prominence during the siba period. Today it is the largest of the wlad siyyed groups, and, more importantly, it is the one sublineage in

Sidi Lahcen which has managed to achieve a high degree of unity. It is the only such unified group in the village.

The prominence of the Ait Ghazi ben Allal sublineage at the beginning of the Protectorate period was a function of the prestige of the Moqaddem Hamid as well as the demise of the Ait Sidi Mohammed. As the Protectorate period progressed, the basis of power shifted and this sublineage was not assured continued affluence. Its members responded by solidifying through common action, endogamy, and avoidance of feuds, and thus greatly increased their power and position. Their ability to act collectively was a major factor in forestalling the rise of powerful individuals.

In this sublineage there are five extended families who maintain common hearths, common expenses, and undivided inheritance. There are no other examples of common hearths in the rest of the Ait Sidi Hamid lineage. This mutual confidence and trust has enabled them to practice a division of labor. One of the men is thus free to engage in nonfarming activity which assures additional income for the group. Such cooperation has enabled the sublineage to acquire a proportionally greater amount of land both in the core area and in the secondary area.

The members of the Ait Ghazi ben Allal live clustered around one of the main springs, and their houses form a tight compound snuggled together at the end of the central village area. They pride themselves on their public demeanor and on their practice of not loitering in the stores which surround the flat *musem* area where other villagers gather to drink tea, gossip, and gamble. They have distributed their properties evenly; no individual in this group has achieved great personal wealth or power, because attempts to obtain such power have been successfully thwarted by group action.

During each of the historical periods this sublineage demonstrates the most successful way of making the system work: in the period of siba, the Moqaddem Hamid exemplified the values of mediator and attracted great prestige and power to himself and to his brothers; during the Protectorate, the Ait Ghazi ben Allal enlarged its economic base by acting as a group, thus ensuring its own material stability and welfare; finally, in the Independence period, the members of the sublineage were the most assertive in attaining positions outside of the village when this proved to be valuable.

The second sublineage of the Ait Sidi Hamid—the Ait ben Shedli— has also played an important role in village life and will provide a useful counterimage to the Ait Ghazi ben Allal. Second in size among the wlad siyyed groups, the Ait ben Shedli commanded a strong economic and social position at the end of siba. The trajectory of its fortunes during the Protectorate period fell, however, much as those of the Ait Ghazi ben Allal continued to rise. Its members fought incessantly amongst themselves, and their divisiveness was crucial. One of them—the religious judge Si Jelloul—through his connection to the French and through his role as qadi, was able to achieve great wealth during the Protectorate. Although he bought no land in Sidi Lahcen itself, he systematically acquired large numbers of olive trees. His brothers exhausted their energies for thirty years in futile scheming to siphon off his wealth. The results, over the span of a generation, were disastrous for the whole group.

The Ait ben Shedli stand in marked contrast to the Ait Ghazi ben Allal in their dispersed residence pattern. During the time of siba, all the villagers moved closer together for protection. When the French ended siba, the Ait Ghazi ben Allal continued to remain solidary and consolidate their holdings, whereas the Ait ben Shedli scattered and fought among themselves.

Position is what you make of it; both of these sublineages were in the same structural position within the village. Wlad siyyed, they shared the same opportunities, but not the same fates.

The wlad abad, literally "descendants of the slaves," claim to have been the inhabitants of the village area when Sidi Lahcen arrived there in the seventeenth century. Their origins, however, are rather obscure. One tale suggests that they came from the Gharb; another that they originated from the Missour area (Sidi Lahcen's homeland) and that they had migrated into the lower Middle Atlas. One lineage, so the story goes, moved down, established itself in its present location, and was followed by several other groups from the same area. Even in this version the various lineages do not claim common descent or affiliation (except geographically). Yet another version traces their descent back to the original slaves of Sidi Lahcen at Tamgrut, who migrated north with the saint. As a matter of fact, there is a group of wlad abad who are distinctly darker in skin color than other villagers. In any case, the wlad abad are an amalgam of groups who came to Sidi Lahcen over an extended period of time and who were socially defined under the common rubric of wlad abad, a clear marker to set them off from the wlad siyyed. They themselves lament their unknown origins, *assal*, and see it as one of their great misfortunes.

While it is true that some of the wlad siyyed sublineages were divisive and extremely noncohesive, they did have an ideology of belonging to a distinct group whose origins and genealogical unity were clear. They were sure that they were members of a group even if they did not want to have anything to do with the other members of their sublineage. Not so for the wlad abad. Internally they have neither unity nor disunity; they are not a group. Viewed externally, however, they have been given the common name of wlad abad; this specifies them as non-wlad siyyed inhabitants of the area who have accepted Sidi Lahcen as *mul bled*, the saint of the land.

Whatever their origins, the wlad abad were, by the beginning of the Protectorate, no longer a defined series of lineages but rather a collection of separate families. Their inability to act as a group left them extremely vulnerable.

The wlad abad live, for the most part, adjacent to each other in houses spread out along the upper section of the neutral musem area, but they have no central focus for group activity. They manifest neither the explosion of the Ait ben Shedli nor the implosion of the Ait Ghazi ben Allal, but rather a less intense dispersion.[1]

These three collectivities may be classified as follows: (1) a highly unified, endogamous, and prosperous sublineage; (2) a sublineage which has been torn by strife and has never been able to give its group identity a workable social form or to prevent the rise of powerful individuals; (3) a collectivity which bears a common name but has not been a group at all.

The three groups have three quite distinct marriage patterns: one highly endogamous, one less so, and the third not at all. But all three operate according to the same principles, both in terms of conscious considerations and in the working out of latent or indirect processes.

All of my informants, wlad siyyed and non-wlad siyyed alike, emphasized that the most important consideration in marriage was the character of the future in-laws. One marries the bride's father, they say, but also her mother, brothers, and sisters. The success of marriage will depend on how the in-laws get along with each other. The main thing to consider is whether the bride's family will interfere in the affairs of the couple.

Much of the literature on the Arab North African world stresses a normative preference for marriage to the father's brother's daughter— preferential patrilateral parallel cousin marriage. When I questioned the villagers about this, however, it was clear that they thought about marital agreements in very different terms. The structural position of the bride was not the point. The reputation of the bride's family and the quality of the interpersonal relations between her family and that of the bridegroom was the prime consideration. Some of the discussion on Arabic marriage patterns has argued that the choice of a patrilateral parallel cousin is likely to insure that the property of two brothers will not be dispersed through inheritance but rather consolidated. Islamic inheritance includes the wife as well as the children. This leads to the possibility that the property will pass out of the patrilineal line through the female inheritors. But, in practice, there are innumerable ways to avoid female inheritance; it does not turn out to be a problem for this form of marriage in Morocco.

Fragmentation of land holdings through inheritance by agnates, however, is a real problem. Few men in the village have a single large field of even three hectares in size, and most have many tiny holdings in different places. The average size of the holdings in the irrigated core area is four-fifths of a hectare. This kind of extreme fragmentation has been avoided only by one subgroup in the village, the Ait Ghazi ben Allal, who have not divided up their inheritance but work it as a family.

The consolidation of landholdings is probably not a single consequence of lineage endogamy. The crucial variable is the degree of cohesiveness characteristic of this group of close kinsmen. The cohesiveness makes possible economic cooperation and repeated intermarriage which in turn reinforce the cohesiveness. There is no single factor at work here, but rather a complex systematic interaction which brings about a "family tradition of solidarity."

Attitudes toward the possibilities of marital choice vary. When questioned, the young men from the Ait Ghazi ben Allal said that they married a girl from their own sublineage because they knew her family, who were close relatives, and they knew that they could get along with them. This is basic. Structural gymnastics are not. Another informant, this one from the Ait ben Shedli sublineage, whose divisiveness, bickering, and backstabbing are as much their hallmark as are the cooperativeness, caution, and helpfulness of the Ait Ghazi ben Allal, said that what matters most in marriage are the in-laws. Because his sublineage mates were so difficult to get along with and so untrustworthy, he would not marry his relatives because that would mean certain trouble. To emphasize and legitimate his point, he quoted a saying of the prophet, "If you marry, marry far away."

The crux of the calculation on the part of the man and his family is their probable relationship with the girl's family. Getting married is an investment and takes years of planning and preparation. A girl who will return to her family after a fight is a very bad investment. People say that getting a girl back from her family once she has returned to them is like getting remarried. If your sublineage mates are people you can get along with, then it is preferable to marry endogamously, but if they are not, the advantages of endogamy are outweighed by its disadvantages. As one old man put it, "Marriage is like prospecting, you have to dig around a lot before you find gold. The gold is more important than where you find it."

THREE MEN, THREE STRATEGIES

The dynamics of the strategies of the three groups become clearer if we examine the careers of three influential villagers, one from each of the groups. Individual action, group strategy, and the historical situation may thus all be shown as dimensions of the same phenomenon.

Abadi—"un grand seigneur." The first man from Sidi Lahcen who managed to forge his connections with the French into powerful advantage was the qadi Abadi from the wlad abad. He grew up in Fez and not in the village itself, because his father had been subjected to harsh treatment by the qaid of Zgan during the siba period and so had moved out to Fez. The son, however, maintained a keen interest in his natal village.

Abadi attended the famous Qarawiyin University in Fez and then was appointed qadi (religious judge), in Sefrou. After this post he was to have an illustrious career holding qadi positions in major cities throughout Morocco. By the end of the Protectorate he was moving in the highest political circles in the kingdom, those around the Glawi.

Abadi was an extremely gregarious man, yet an astute politician, who lived in the ostentatious style of the *grands seigneurs,* so dear to foreign travelers in Morocco. He was extremely hospitable, fond of entertaining and distributing presents. His houses in Sefrou and Fez were always open to villagers who came to receive food and small favors. He had an elaborate network of political connections throughout Morocco and was at ease in the old-style politics which combined lavish redistribution with ruthless use of power. For these reasons he is remembered in the village with the deep ambivalence which usually surrounds powerful figures of this type. He was greatly feared by the villagers but also held in awe, especially for his generosity. One old man compared this type of powerful figure to a cow: "They come and eat your crops but later you get some milk in return."

Upon graduating in 1920, Abadi requested and successfully attained a position as qadi in the religious court in Sefrou. Through his position he had access to the land deeds for the region and for Sidi Lahcen in particular. Having the French behind him, he was quite free to do as he wished. In his first years as qadi he did not interfere with, and actually maintained an active and sympathetic interest in, his lineage mates and village affairs in general. Suddenly, however, at the end of his tenure as qadi, he reversed himself and confiscated the major portion of the land of his lineage mates as well as many of their olive trees. He did it rapidly, brutally, and efficiently. He then left the Sefrou area to take up other posts.

One day Abadi appeared in the village with a French agricultural engineer who had come, he told the villagers, to survey the land in order to establish proper land deeds. Abadi had the maps drawn; they indicated that he was the owner of the major portion of the best land of the wlad abad, including practically all of their irrigated land. Of a total of fifty-five hectares of land that members of the wlad abad owned, he took nineteen. The wlad abad today, more than thirty-five years later, have still not recovered. Abadi also acquired through similar means some sixteen hundred olive trees. This is eight times as many trees as anyone else owns in the village and 8 percent of all the trees in the village.

Abadi did not restrict himself to taking land from the wlad abad, although interestingly enough most of what he took did come from them. He also took land from people in the other village clusters, and even a plot from the Ait Ghazi ben Allal sublineage.

He acquired most of the land by the resurveying trick. People say that they knew what was happening but that either they were paid to keep silent or they were intimidated. Those whose fields were being stolen were helpless. They saw and understood that when the qadi, the courts, and the French combined in an action, there was really nothing the individual could do. As one old man put it, when a large truck is coming down the road, you get out of the way.

Abadi also lent money to villagers, demanding trees or land as collateral. Once he had control of the deeds, the land was his. Two attempts were made to thwart Abadi. A delegation of wlad siyyed went to Sefrou and told him that what he was doing was *haram* and *hashuma*, immoral and shameful. His response was to bribe several other villagers to come to Sefrou and testify in court that he, Abadi, owned one of the fields of the wlad siyyed; the warning was unambiguous. The only other attempt to stop him had more drastic consequences. Another member of the wlad siyyed started to criticize Abadi openly. One night the man was killed; Abadi took possession of his fields, and opposition ceased.

Perhaps the most interesting question, and one for which I have no answer, is why the qadi Abadi stopped when he did. There were no obvious restraints on his power in this sphere. He seems to have calculated the amount of land he wanted, planned how to acquire it, taken it, and then left the Sefrou area. Nevertheless, he maintained relations with many of the villagers throughout his whole life and kept himself informed on village affairs.

The actions of the qadi Abadi brought misery to a generation of wlad abad. The thin margin of economic security which they had been maintaining was obliterated in a stroke. Once a large portion of their land was taken, their impoverished position made them vulnerable to losing other parts of their holdings. For example, in 1945, a year of terrible drought in Morocco, one of the men from the wlad abad sold his last remaining field for four bags of chick-peas.

The effects of Abadi on the wlad abad have been devastating and will probably be felt for at least another generation. Although his economic impact on the rest of the village has been minimal, he serves as a much discussed model of unchallengeable power which the villagers associate with the central government. People say, "A man should fear Allah and men like the qadi Abadi."

Jelloul—slow and legal. The second man from Sidi Lahcen to attend the Qarawiyin university was Si Jelloul of the Ait ben Shedli sublineage. He also became a powerful qadi, although never as influential as Abadi, and he too had an important effect on the village. Si Jelloul is a sort of countermodel to Abadi. Abadi was *haram*, unlawful, but he was also generous, political in the largest sense, and outgoing. Jelloul was lawful in his dealings with the villagers to the point of scrupulous honesty, but he was a tight-lipped, inhospitable, nonpolitical, and generally disagreeable man.

Abadi left the wlad abad impoverished. Jelloul's impact was of a rather different sort. Many of his brothers, forming the core of the Ait ben Shedli sublineage, spent their lives scheming among one another in vain attempts to steal, or at least to insure for themselves the inheritance of, Si Jelloul's wealth. In the process, they not only failed to secure this wealth but actually lost the majority of their own holdings.

Si Jelloul never acquired any land in Sidi Lahcen itself, although he used his position to get large holdings in another area of Morocco. He did, however, acquire some six hundred olive trees in the village, second only to Abadi. People say that Jelloul was a very honest qadi, as qadi-s go, but even the most honest qadi acquired great wealth from the office.

Jelloul visited Sidi Lahcen twice each year, once at the fall musem and once at the olive harvest. During these visits he acquired his olive trees (all in the core area on irrigated land). It was well known in the village that Jelloul would pay cash for trees in the core area. In this rather patient and systematic manner he gradually built up his substantial holdings. Only during the famine year of 1945 did he buy a large number of trees.

It was from his brothers that he acquired the very first trees, and they spent the rest of their lives trying to get them back. One of the brothers was delegated to care for the trees and supervise their handling and was even initially delegated to buy trees for Si Jelloul. Although he was rewarded with one-quarter of the harvest each year—an ample sum—the man was not satisfied and attempted to register all of Si Jelloul's trees in his own name. He was rebuffed, naturally enough, at the court by Si Jelloul's colleagues and was dismissed as caretaker, thereby losing his entire income. Another brother appointed several years later, attempted a similar maneuver with similar results. The constant fighting and thieving of the sublineage reached such a height that no one willingly could be made the caretaker.

A third brother followed Si Jelloul to another area of Morocco where he had extensive holdings. Although this brother seems to have been more upright, he never received more than a modest salary for his efforts. Two other brothers also followed Si Jelloul around Morocco assisting him in various ways and attempting, if unsuccessfully, to swindle him and others.

The poorest brother of all, who was also the most religious, did not try to cheat Jelloul or ask favors from him. Toward the end of his life Jelloul entrusted this man with increasingly heavy responsibilities but few rewards. The man's hope was not for great wealth for himself, but merely that Jelloul would set his son up in a bureaucratic post. Unfortunately for the son, Jelloul died in a bus accident shortly after his appointment in Fez, and no post was made available to the boy.

While the qadi Abadi openly stole land and trees as his lineage mates suffered impotently, the qadi Si Jelloul performed no technically illegal actions against anyone in the village. He made his real fortune elsewhere through his position as qadi in another region of Morocco. His sublineage mates, however, spent their lives in a vain quest for his wealth. Jelloul, who, as the villagers say, was strong (*shih*) with the government, foiled them at all turns; this led them on to greater and more reckless excesses and even greater defeat. So this sublineage, which had been well off at the end of siba, was now highly factional and discordant, having lost most of what it once had.

Mohammed bel Ghazi: a counterexample. Mohammed bel Ghazi was from the Ait Ghazi ben Allal sublineage. Whereas the height of the qadi Abadi's activity was during the 1920s and '30s, and Si Jelloul's during the 1930s through the '50s, bel Ghazi was an important force from the 1940s through the '60s. These dates are important because bel Ghazi self-consciously and explicitly tried to imitate the methods of the qadi Abadi. By the closing years of the Protectorate, however, these methods were not nearly as effective as they once had been. The French had begun to institute a series of structural reforms in a vain attempt to save their Protectorate, and the Moroccans had grown more sophisticated in their understanding and use of the French-supported institutions.

Ghazi was a failure and thus an instructive negative example. Although he did not attend the Qarawiyin, he was literate. Because of his abilities he was appointed, as a young man, to be the assistant to Sheikh ben Nasr. The position of sheikh is roughly equivalent to the subgovernor, under the qaid, of an area. The French had appointed the Moqaddem Hamid as the first sheikh. He had acted primarily as an intermediary between the French and the tribesmen. Moqaddem Hamid's son succeeded him during the first two decades of the Protectorate. He was a man of *niya*, character, and highly respected although not very forceful. As he aged, he was less able to cope with his duties, and they were gradually usurped by his assistant, bel Ghazi, who was young, dynamic, and ambitious. Having carefully observed the methods of the qadi Abadi, he intended to duplicate them.

There were two major differences, however, which distinguished bel Ghazi's situation from that of Abadi. First, even when he became sheikh (after World War II), this position was a much weaker one than that of qadi. It did not have direct French support as did the courts, and more importantly, it was still deeply entwined in regional affairs. This difference, as bel Ghazi was to find out, was decisive. Second, he was from the Ait Ghazi ben Allal sublineage—an extremely tightly-knit group whose members themselves had been fearful onlookers to the deeds of the qadi Abadi. Every move that bel Ghazi made was met by a solid counterattack. This solidarity proved vital in land disputes. The procedure in such cases is for the courts to send investigators, paid for by the disputants, to the village to examine the problem. These investigators assemble witnesses; each side has the right to bring forward its own. As we have seen, this system can be circumvented by simply overwhelming it in the way the qadi Abadi did, by having enough money and power to bribe or intimidate all witnesses.

Bel Ghazi tried, with scant success, to reduplicate these methods for thirty years. He was successfully thwarted because, each time he brings a case against his lineage mates, they stand firm and assemble witnesses to validate their claims. Further, they are sufficiently prosperous to pay the court costs.

The first person from whom bel Ghazi attempted to steal some land was his father. His father had bought a field from one of the wlad abad. Several years later, bel Ghazi stole the deed and paid some witnesses to testify in Sefrou that the land was his. Since his father was alive, it was impossible that he could have inherited it, and the court ruled against him, sending him to jail for a short period. When he was released, he convinced his father that they should jointly borrow money from the French for agricultural improvements and put up the deed as collateral. Bel Ghazi then paid off the debt, receiving the deed in return. When his father died, he claimed that the land was his. The other legitimate inheritors banded together assembled witnesses and lawyers, and won their case. Bel Ghazi was foiled several times in this fashion.

Tactics of this kind have, however, worked with other groups in the village. Bel Ghazi took all the land of a man from the wlad abad who could not get anyone in the village to serve as a witness for him and who could not afford the costs involved. He stole a large sum from a man who had been sending money back from the army. The money was to be used to purchase land, and indeed it was: bel Ghazi bought the land but put his own name on the deed.

Although he has managed to collect some fifteen hectares of land by employing these methods, most of his attempts have been blocked. He had no solid base of support. He was not a man to be taken lightly, he was the sheikh, but he was not quite powerful enough to overcome the unity that was used to counter him.

During the Protectorate, power and well-being centered on the acquisition of land and trees. As the functions of the wlad siyyed were undermined and their economic position was undercut, land became more valuable. The Ait Ghazi ben Allal emerged during this period as the most successful sublineage. Its members acted together, married endogamously, avoided divorce, and lived clustered together. This unity enabled them to increase their resources, acquire more land and trees, and successfully defend themselves against bel Ghazi, who tried to use the wider system to improve his own position at their expense.

5. The Culture of Politics

Perceptions and Conflict

Political activity of a diverse and complex sort has dominated village life since the beginning of the Second World War. During the course of the war, village perceptions of the French underwent a basic modification. This change was occasioned both by French confiscation policies, which humiliated and exploited the villagers, and by the contact with the American army. In wealth and demeanor the Americans contrasted strongly with the French, who now for the first time were perceived as vulnerable.

NEW PERCEPTIONS

Despite the far-reaching structural changes brought about by the French Protectorate, the villagers had had little face-to-face contact with French administrators. From the Protectorate's inception, the French had used local institutions (or what they believed to be such) to mediate between themselves and the Moroccans. French "visibility" in the countryside was kept to a minimum and local officials were usually Moroccan. After the proposed military academy had been rejected by the village, villagers can remember only two major incidents of direct French intervention in their day-to-day affairs.

First, for a short period in the 1930s when the large French "colon" farms were having severe economic problems, the villagers were drafted to work as farm laborers. This operation was supervised by a Moroccan official, who conducted it in a brutal manner. The villagers particularly resented the coercive fashion in which the project was presented to them and the demeaning treatment they received. This never became an institutionalized policy, however, and it is remembered as an unpleasant incident not typical of French rule.

A second incident of French interference concerned an attempt to introduce a modern mill into the village. All agreed that the mill would benefit the village, that there was a real need for it. But as the French were trying to force it on them *b-s-sif*, "by the sword," the villagers could not accept it. The French, uncomprehendingly, backed down. They had conceived the project in a utilitarian fashion but had presented it in a mandatory form. Despite their self-styled sophistication and the "progressive" policies they prided themselves on, the French officials never seemed to have gained a real comprehension of Moroccan culture.

The Moroccans began to see the French in a new light during the war years. It was really during this period that the independence movement began (at least in rural perceptions of these events). Two sets of experiences were central here: those of the men in the army and those of the men who remained in Sidi Lahcen. For this second group, who were the vast majority, the French policy of confiscation of oil and grain, and especially the manner in which it was carried out, was the turning point.

Due to grave shortages, the French were forced to appropriate food to feed their own army. The quotas fixed for the village were not unbearably high and by themselves probably would have been tolerated. The French, however, administered the program through the local Moroccan officials, who, with the tacit approval of French administrators, looted the countryside, causing open and deep hatred. The image of the French, which had been somewhat undefined previously, darkened. Whatever minimal legitimacy they had painstakingly constructed was rapidly dissipated. This is not to imply that rural Morocco turned into a guerilla base, but rather that these policies began a process of basic reevaluation of the French, a resymbolization.

The enforced passivity, the house-to-house searches, and the insults are still bitterly remembered twenty-five years later. The years of careful avoidance of encroachment on daily life were negated. The perceptions of the French which were being formed in these years were to be reinforced by other political activity after the war.

Contact with the American army in North Africa and Italy during the Second World War was also instrumental in altering the perceptions of what Christians were or might be. In this case, the generosity and seemingly unlimited wealth of the American forces contrasted rather strikingly to the French condition. Further, the lack of an emphasis on symbols of hierarchy (again in contrast to the French) deeply impressed the Moroccan soldiers. These shifts in perceptions provided a form, a down-to-earth model, by means of which the worldwide and national structural changes could be made concrete and meaningful. My argument is not that such changes in evaluation were causal, but rather that they were an important dimension of the on-going process of decolonization. They were a basic mode of bringing the macrochanges down to the scale of everyday life and known values. It is in this way that they could become a source of political action.

While the French were confiscating the oil and grain of villagers, the Americans were feeding and supplying themselves, their allies, and even, it seemed, their enemies. The tremendous affluence and waste of the American army had a profound impact on those villagers who witnessed it. As one man put it, "The Americans threw away more equipment and food than the French had for their whole army." The sheer bounty was overwhelming.

Secondly, the minimization of external, symbolically expressed hierarchy in the American forces also deeply impressed the Moroccans. In sharp contrast to the French, American officers wore uniforms similar to those of their men, and there was much public bantering and joking. The officers often did manual labor, pushed jeeps, etc. More important perhaps, the American soldiers, both officers and enlisted men, treated the Moroccans without protocol, in an unreserved and generous manner, freely distributing food and supplies.

For the Moroccans, the Americans exemplified—unlike the French —virtues which are central to the Moroccan value system: *shih* (strength), *karim* (generosity), and even-handedness. The generosity of the Moqaddem Hamid, as we have seen, was not only the substance but the proof of his baraka. His even-handed giving demonstrated that he was the best of men and favored by Allah, as manifested by the yield from his land, consumed by the people. This is not to say that the Americans were seen as having baraka, but their generosity was greatly valued, and it cast an uncomplimentary light on the French.

The manner of giving was also quite important. A common response to a "thank you" in Morocco is to say *bla jmil*—without obligation, there is no necessity to reciprocate, the affair is well finished, the favor will not be publicly vaunted. This completes the context in which the Americans' behavior was perceived. Their giving was done, so it seemed, for its own sake; hence it was something astonishing and respected. While one should be extremely cautious in drawing conclusions from these data, comments about the American mode of giving have been made time and time again by Moroccans.

The other quality mentioned was that of *shih*, which is a core symbol in Moroccan culture. There is a basic opposition between strength, force, power (*shih*), and weakness, enervation, fatigue (*ayyan*), which permeates all of the cultural life of the village. It is a primary standard used in judging. A man may be shih, or his animals, or his health, or his crops, or a point in an argument, or the rain, or a meal—virtually anything—and the same things also may be weak, tired, ayyan. Shih is not restricted to physical strength or weakness but is broader, deeper, and more encompassing, indicating "full of life and its vitality"; and the process of increasing and strengthening these qualities. This processual dimension of increase, filling—or its reverse —is a central part of the symbol. To be shih has a double connotation: the presence of this vitality and its increase and deepening.

Something that is shih is good, not necessarily in the sense that it is correct or proper, but in the sense that it is vital and is blessed by Allah. To say something is shih is to admire it, to acknowledge the power of Allah, which often goes beyond the human powers of understanding. Much as with baraka, increase, plenitude, and vigor are considered the substance and expression of Allah's majesty. Shih, however, is a broader symbol that is not given the same explicit religious elaboration as baraka. It is more primary than baraka, a quality of being that one stands in awe of, a quality that is in itself worthy of respect. This aspect of shih is important. The power of the early qaid-s, for example, was something one respected even if one detested them. Their power was proof on a deep level of their divine favor; its decrease or disappearance signified the withdrawal of that favor. This does not mean that Moroccans acquiesced to exploitation by the qaid-s or "fatalistically" saw the hand of Allah. It does mean that there was an added dimension of fear and respect for such men. These powerful figures had obviously been favored by Allah for some reason—perhaps because of their strength. The awe in which they were held, however, lasted as long as their strength. Qadi Abadi and the French were considered to be shih. Abadi's acts were condemned and scorned time and again. Yet there was always a hint of admiration for the undeniable fact of his strength, his success. Shih is always admired even in the most unacceptable actions.

It is a quality, however, which by its very nature invites comparisons. If a man is shih, one fears him; if another man comes along with a better quip, a larger horse, or a bigger army, then the first man is no longer shih, he is ayyan. This is what happened during the war. The French, once powerful and mighty, were suddenly seen to be ayyan. The fear and respect which the French had elicited because of their strength was undercut; their force and vitality were decreasing and their vulnerability was increasing. Whereas they were undertaking a program of confiscation which led to both privation and humiliation, they were now seen as not being totally strong and powerful. Their power was relativized, and this, combined with the deep resentment bred by humiliation, set the stage for the political challenges which followed the war.

Conflict in the period immediately preceding Independence centered on confrontations over symbols of identity. By the end of that period, the villagers seemed to have attained a culturally dominant position. It was an illusion, however, since regional political networks and power balances had shifted. As the villagers had again failed to establish meaningful political relations in those wider networks, their positions, in fact, had been further undermined by their own actions.

EXILE OF THE SULTAN

Following the war, political power in the Sidi Lahcen region was crystallized around the figures of two powerful qaid-s. The first, Qaid Larbi, became a strong supporter of the French and in return received aid from them. Larbi had been a benefactor of the wlad siyyed even though they were not technically under his jurisdiction. He had aided them during the confiscations of the war years and the disastrous drought of 1945. Later, he had even established a market in the village which he intended to expand into a regional economic center. Among his own tribesmen, Larbi was notorious for his coercive and brutal manner, but with the wlad siyyed his behavior was entirely the reverse. He respected the wlad siyyed because they were shurfa, he often proclaimed, and he wanted to help them. His actions consistently followed his rhetoric. Since his aid was not b-s-sif, and since it flattered and reinforced their identity, the wlad siyyed accepted his offer of a market.

The other powerful qaid was Lahcen Lyussi in Sefrou. He was the qaid for the Ait Yussi and organized and led the guerilla liberation army which operated during the sultan's exile. He seems to have been hostile to the wlad siyyed; in any case he was perceived as such. It is reported that he spoke condescendingly about the wlad siyyed calling them "only shurfa," implying that they were not as manly as the Berbers.

When the sultan Mohammed V was exiled by the French in 1953, the wlad siyyed found themselves caught in a contradictory situation. Despite their wishes, they were aligned with Qaid Larbi. He had been their strong supporter, and they were associated with him in the eyes of others. In general, however, they did not take the same political positions he did. They depended on the sultan for their own legitimation and they had especially strong emotional ties with Mohammed V. Opposing the sultan's exile was Qaid Lyussi, who was hostile to the wlad siyyed but whose politics were closer to those of most of the villagers. This bind, combined with the traditional stance of political neutrality, was one of the major reasons that the villagers avoided political activity and overt political alignment during the exile of the sultan.

The consequences of the French move were unavoidable, however, and despite themselves the wlad siyyed were involved in a series of confrontations. The first were symbolic ones. Every Friday there is a communal prayer at the mosque in Sidi Lahcen. In this prayer the name of the sultan is pronounced. He is the imam of the Moroccan Muslim community, and reciting his name is an indication of submission to his spiritual leadership, a validation of his right to rule. When the French deposed Mohammed V, Qaid Larbi sent an order to all the villages under his jurisdiction, including Sidi Lahcen, requiring that the new sultan's name be used in the prayer. The *fqi*, koranic teacher, of the mosque in Sidi Lahcen, with the approval of the majority of the villagers, refused to comply. When the time came for him to pronounce the name of the new puppet sultan, he simply coughed over it. This was defiance, but it fell far short of the open rebellion which had occurred elsewhere in Morocco.

Qaid Larbi, upon hearing of this, came to the village and publicly threatened the fqi. The following Friday the fqi again coughed over the name, and a new man was sent to replace him. On the next day the new man received a threatening note; he fled. In a rage, Larbi returned to the village. Assembling the entire village, he demanded to know who had sent the letter, and he threatened dire consequences if the man was not caught. The villagers maintained a solid and silent front. In total frustration and so as not to appear totally foolish, Larbi jailed the old caretaker of the mosque. Another new fqi was sent to the village; he did not last long either. No one would feed him or come to the mosque. He left after several days. Finally, Larbi relented and ordered the return of the original fqi.

On this initial confrontation, the village (wlad siyyed and non-wlad siyyed alike) had stood together. They had resolutely refused to affirm, even verbally, an illegitimate sultan. The issue had been kept on a muted level, however, by their not insisting on pronouncing the name of Mohammed V, which would have been an open and defiant political act.

Villagers remained united on a second confrontation with Qaid Larbi. The sultan had been exiled during the month of Ramadan, which is followed two months later by the holiday of *aid l-kbir*, perhaps the most important religious celebration of the year. This is usually a feast day and a time of rejoicing. The villagers refused to celebrate the aid; they said that they felt "as if in mourning" and that it would be inappropriate and disrespectful to hold a festival. They wore old clothes and almost no one sacrificed a sheep. Hearing this, Larbi again came to the village. He assembled the villagers and asked who had celebrated the aid l-kbir. The chorus of positive replies only infuriated him more, and he demanded to see the sheepskins from the freshly slaughtered sheep. Most of the villagers remained assembled and began chanting, "hashuma, hashuma," literally, "shame on you," "scandalous behavior." Larbi became extremely agitated, obviously confused and disturbed by his own position. Suddenly he begged the pardon of the wlad siyyed and left the village.

Qaid Larbi was not a man who backed down very often, but in this case, he seems to have been restrained by respect for the wlad siyyed and also, perhaps, by fear of the saint.

Although the villagers had presented a united front behind the wlad siyyed in these confrontations over core symbols, they were rather less united on other political issues. From the very beginning of the period preceding Independence, there had been informers in Sidi Lahcen who worked secretly for Larbi and the French. These same men might display solidarity on the symbolic issues and also hedge their bets by working for the French. Possibilities of gain, through such a powerful ally, still tempted many villagers. Bel Ghazi, whom we discussed earlier, is an outstanding example.

There were both wlad siyyed and non-wlad siyyed among the French supports. Even within the Ait Ghazi ben Allal, whom we have taken as a model of solidarity, there were several men who were pro-French. In this situation, desire for adventure or gain, individual courage or its lack, and personal feuds were the relevant variables.

Although many wlad siyyed advocated political neutrality, a strong anti-French faction began to form in the village. It was spurred by the imposition of security measures, which sustained the very attitudes and actions they had been instituted to prevent—sabotage and anti-

French feeling. The French succeeded in creating an atmosphere of tension, divisiveness, political factionalism, and fear.

A bitter and open hostility developed within the village during the years of the sultan's exile. The leaders of the anti-French forces, led by a non-wlad siyyed named Ali, actively and successfully worked at isolating the group of French supporters, at great risk to themselves. In fact, most of them were arrested during the period. By the end of the second year of the exile, the children of the pro-French faction had been ostracized by the other children. Hostilities between factions in the village, however, never reached a point of physical violence or, for that matter, of sabotage of property. At their limit they consisted in an economic boycott directed against a storekeeper who was eventually driven out of the village. He moved to a nearby village, to which he was followed by a man from the Ait ben Shedli who organized the villagers there against this man until he was again forced to move. Only after a seven-year exile could he return to Sidi Lahcen.

Beginning in 1953, and continuing until the return of the sultan, the anti-French groups carried out a policy of sabotage. There was no murder in this region, and most of the sabotage activity consisted in burning French farms, cutting telephone wires, and the like. Villagers stress that they were not against the French per se but were engaging only in activity aimed at forcing the return of the sultan. Leaders of this movement, who enjoyed reliving their adventures, indignantly denied having harassed the French schoolteachers. They said that would have been *hashuma*, inappropriate and scandalous.

When terrorist activity began, there were false reports sent to Qaid Larbi that the leaders were living in Sidi Lahcen. An order was sent to the sheikh, a grandson of the Moqaddem Hamid, to produce the men or face jail himself. He refused, disclaiming all knowledge, and was removed from office and even jailed for a short time. He was replaced by a man from a neighboring village who was openly anti-wlad siyyed. This only aggravated the situation, did not stop the terrorism, and further crystallized the anti-French sentiment. Eventually the original sheikh was released and reinstated. Throughout the duration of the exile, he refused to cooperate with the French or Qaid Larbi, but he did act as an intermediary between various factions. He maintained an active neutrality.

The musem was banned during this period, which only added to the sense of "unnaturalness." Nineteen fifty-five was an extremely bad agricultural year in the region. Several elders of the Ait Yussi petitioned Qaid Larbi for permission to hold the saint's festival. After some hesitation, he agreed. On the second night of the musem, a bomb was thrown into Qaid Larbi's tent but failed to explode. A cook who had seen the bomb thrower refused to identify him. (Villagers say that she had been more afraid of Sidi Lahcen that of Qaid Larbi.) The musem was promptly canceled.

In addition to this loosely organized and individualistic sabotage, a national guerrilla army, organized and led by Qaid Lahcen Lyussi in Sefrou, was active in the region. Only one man from Sidi Lahcen joined the army, but several others served as liaison men and many villagers offered at least tacit support.

During the initial stages of the exile, the army was constantly on the move deep in the Middle Atlas forests. But toward the end of the exile period, it established bases close to Sidi Lahcen. From the very beginnings of its operations, the army had kept accounts of enemies and supporters. At the end of the independence struggle, when it controlled much of the Middle Atlas and had a virtual monopoly of force in the area, it exacted vengeance on many opponents. The friendships and aliiances formed in the army of liberation proved to be instrumental in the political structure of the region after Independence. This was not the case within the village. The pro- and anti-French factions did not solidify into groups and have not proved to be a basis for on-going political affiliations.

This period of cacophonous tensions, sabotage, intrigue, confrontations, informers, and liberation armies ended rather abruptly with the return to Morocco of the exiled sultan in 1955. Upon returning, he issued a plea for unity; his enemies should be forgiven and the fighting should stop. His call had immediate effect in the countryside. Few reprisals (at least in the village) were taken, and the prolonged and ecstatic celebration, combined with the sultan's wise policy of forgiveness and unification, ended the period harmoniously.

The situation of the exile was seen as one of abnormality, with no sultan, no musem. The sultan himself echoed this theme upon his return, saying the exile was an unfortunate episode and should be forgotten. During the exile, the wlad siyyed had united to assert and protect their cultural identity against those who challenged it, but failed again to perceive and act upon new alliances, power bases, and political structures which were forming in the region. Again the price they were to pay for maintaining their identity was the loss of concrete material satisfactions and prosperity. They were soon made aware of this.

POLITICAL FAILURE: THE LOSS OF THE RURAL CENTER

Independence was achieved in 1956, the year following the sultan's return from exile, and with it came a more routinized form of politics. Along with a general sense of elation and high expectations of great and wonderful change—which the *Istiqlal*, Independence, party had promised—came an immediate effort to gain control over offices throughout the country. Within the region of Sidi Lahcen these activities centered first on the office of sheikh. The sheikh was a rural official who served under the qaid. During the Protectorate period various curbs had been placed on the position of qaid, although, as exemplified by the qaid-s Larbi and Lyussi, the position could still be powerful and important when filled by a dynamic and assertive man.

After Independence there was a reorganization of the formal political structure in Morocco. One of its explicit goals was consolidation and centralization of power. In line with this aim the position of qaid was weakened. Qaid-s were no longer permitted to hold office in their home territories (until 1972) and were often transferred from post to post. In this way they had little possibility for or interest in building and consolidating a local power base; their knowledge of the region under their actual command was often scant. Today the qaid is seen as an outsider and a rather uninformed one at that. In the qaid's place, other loci of power and influence have arisen in which local "big men," the real power brokers in the region, do not hold office but manipulate and utilize resources through other channels.

These changes have also resulted in an increased importance for the position of sheikh. He is the one government official who lives in the countryside and who is truly informed about rural activities. Formally, his job consists in transmitting decrees and information back and forth from the government to the countryside. Informally, however, he can become a rather powerful figure since he has the authority of the government behind him and because, unlike the official qaid, he is a local man who knows the region well. Rural people complain that they have no check on the sheikh because the qaid believes everything the sheikh tells him. They see the political structure now as vertical, like a ladder, with the sheikh as the bottom rung and information going only in one direction—up—and force going in the other—down. The sheikh, they say, can do as he likes as long as he pleases those above him, because it is he who has the say (literally "the word") with the other government officials. Villagers feel isolated and oppressed by this political situation and have opted, at least in Sidi Lahcen, for a strategy of protective withdrawal. Whereas the sheikh is not as powerful as the qaid was, he is nonetheless potentially dangerous and should be avoided. As we shall see, the villagers choose their own officials to do just that, keep the sheikh distant.

As previously mentioned, Qaid Lahcen Lyussi was antagonistic toward the wlad Sidi Lahcen. After the return of the sultan from his exile and the subsequent granting of independence, Qaid Lyussi emerged as the dominant figure in the region. One of his first moves was to appoint a loyal supporter from the Berber village of Zgan to the position of sheikh. This man, who was still in office in 1969, was hostile toward the wlad siyyed. He immediately appointed Ali, the non-wlad siyyed leader of the local anti-French activity, to be the representative of the village. This move was conceived explicitly as an attack on the wlad siyyed, as Ali was known to resent them. At this time, shortly after Independence, preliminary organization was taking place for what were to become the "rural commune" councils. These elective councils were supposed to be local-level representative bodies which would decide on the implementation of projects for rural improvement—thus involving the rural population in the process of "modernization and nation-building." Because of political maneuvering on the national level the first elections to the councils were delayed until 1960. Ultimately, this delay cost the village dearly because it meant that Ali, who had been appointed by the sheikh, served on the council for the only truly important decision it made.

The location of the new center for the rural commune, which encompassed Sidi Lahcen and the mountain areas around it, was the matter before the council. The logical choice for the center seemed to be Sidi Lahcen, and this time the villagers were eager for modern benefits. Qaid Larbi had chosen Sidi Lahcen as a rural center in the early fifties and had begun to develop it. He had set up and supported a market, and in 1953 he had the French build an elementary school. A survey for a post office, as well as a new road linking the village and Sefrou, had been carried out when the exile of the sultan and the activity surrounding it brought the modernization plans to a halt. Qaid Larbi was driven from office upon the return of the sultan. The villagers of Sidi Lahcen suffered some of the repercussions of his downfall—undeservedly, for they had never really supported him politically and many had actively opposed him, especially on certain key issues. They had accepted the market initially with some reluctance but had been won over by its potential benefits, for which they were becoming increasingly eager.

Exactly how the decision was made is not clear. Ali gives one version and the wlad siyyed another. The result, however, is that Tazutat, an isolated and poor village in the hills north of Sidi Lahcen, is now connected to Sefrou by a tarred road. Tazutat has electricity, a large market, a post office with telephones and government work, and has been transformed into a prospering rural center.

When the decision reached Sidi Lahcen, the villagers and especially the Ait Ghazi ben Allal people were angry. Some of them even went to Rabat, the capital, to petition the ministry, but to no avail. They were told that their representative had signed the document and there was nothing more to be done. Next, a delegation of wlad siyyed went to the qadi Si Jelloul to seek his help. He told them that Sidi Lahcen did not want them to have electricity.

The loss of the center is seen as a turning point by the villagers, in the same way that they now view the Moqaddem Hamid's decision to reject the French offer to build a military school at the beginning of the Protectorate. They feel that if the school had been built, the village would have prospered. They lament being passed over for the rural commune center and complain that it will be another twenty years before they have electricity or even a good road. They feel—rightly— that they have missed their chance for basic economic change for the next generation.

When elections for the rural commune were finally held in 1960, Ali was defeated by a ten-to-one majority. The man who defeated him, Mohammed ben Omar, from the Ait Ghazi ben Allal, is one of the most respected men in the village—he is honest, hard-working, humble, and self-effacing.

There were three elections in the 1960s for the post of commune council representative, and ben Omar won all three by enormous majorities. He was opposed in each election by the same two men: Ali, who vainly tried to mobilize anti-wlad siyyed sentiment, and a wlad siyyed from the Ait Sidi Mohammed. This latter was a very old man and seemed to be living in the past among memories of the time when the Ait Sidi Mohammed were dominant in the village. A neat reflection of sociological forces in voting patterns was skewed in these elections by the fact that Ali was widely considered to be untrust-worthy. He therefore failed to receive support from many villagers even if their sentiments were anti-wlad siyyed. In his attempt to be elected, Ali received strong and open support from the Berber sheikh in Zgan each time but with no success. In the 1969 election he again received only about one-tenth of the vote.

The official duties involved in the position of commune council representative, *moumtil*, included not only participation in the rural commune council, but holding responsibility for handling all official interaction with the government. The moumtil is supposed to function as a countervoice to the sheikh. Although the position is not paid and has little official weight, its importance (as with most positions in Morocco) depends on the man who holds it. Ben Omar was elected because he was honest, quiet, and unassertive. His reelection by such overwhelming margins indicated that the villagers opted for a man who would not cheat them, would not unduly favor any faction, and would not abuse the position. But as one of the wlad siyyed pointed out, the choice also means that nothing will be done for the village, that it will lack forceful representation, that it is likely to be passed over again. A man like Ali would undoubtedly be unfair and untrustworthy, but he would also be more likely to advance (or hurt) the interests of the village. The village has clearly given up hope of government aid and has instead chosen a man who will faithfully report on what happens in the council and who will neither provoke internal problems within the village nor further its interests in the outside world.

TWO MEN ON THEIR OWN: ALI AND CHEF ABDELKRIM

The two men focused on here both gained prominence in the village because of their relations with the French: Ali by fighting against them and Chef Abdelkrim by fighting for them in Indochina and, later, against them in Morocco.

They offer an informative comparison as their methods, resources, and results differed widely. Ali has been, and still is actively involved in all of the major conflicts of the last twenty years. He has attempted to become an important political figure and so far has failed. Chef Abdelkrim, though active in the liberation army, has since refrained from direct political involvement. Yet because of his experiences, which have brought him sustained contact with a much wider world, as well as a large pension from the French, he plays a crucial role in the evolution of the village.

For both men, uncertainties and hesitations about their own identity and about group affiliation—albeit in rather different form— are a central concern. Both have been successful economically but confused and troubled about their cultural situation.

Ali—"always ready." Ali's father moved to Sidi Lahcen at the end of the siba period after the neighboring village of Zera was burned to the ground by a raiding party of Ait Seghrouchen horsemen. He was able to acquire some land in Sidi Lahcen and to establish his family securely. His sons have not had to become agricultural workers and Ali is one of the wealthier men in the village.

Ali has been able to double the two and one half hectares which his father left him, and all the land which he owns is productive. He claims that it is sufficient to meet his needs and that he is not interested in acquiring more. Through the returns from the land he has set up a store, and he has also obtained the government tobacco franchise. His land, store, and the olives he buys at the harvest provide him with what for the village is a substantial income. He is one of those people of whom it is said, *la-bas alih*, things go well with him.

This fact alone makes Ali outstanding, as there are no other men from these splinter factions in the village who have managed to achieve economic success. Ali's initial advantage of having inherited land was complemented by his personal qualities, especially his courage and drive. Toward the end of the Protectorate, as we have seen, he was the leader of the anti-French faction as well as the village head of the *Istiqlal* or Independence party. When questioned about the period, he was reluctant to talk about anything except the adventure involved. He loved to describe in detail how to prepare gasoline bombs and the best techniques for burning fields and cutting telephone lines. His ideological commitments at that time are now blurred and confused in his mind partly, perhaps, because so few of his hopes have come to fruition. He was not against the French, he claimed; he was just for independence. It is important to note, however, that during this period the Istiqlal party called for a tobacco boycott, and Ali, who is known for his stinginess, did participate in the boycott, at great financial loss to himself.

He seems to have been involved for two reasons: because he loved the action and because he hoped to become a "big man." Ali had anticipated that he would be honored as a patriot and rewarded by the government for his actions, but he failed even to receive a government certificate commending his role in the fight. So he felt deceived personally, while the larger-scale changes promised and anticipated in Moroccan society proved even more illusory.

Ali, who had been the first head of the Istiqlal party in the village, felt duped by the political developments after Independence. He was a strong nationalist at the time and faithfully followed the national campaigns of the party. He was unusual in Sidi Lahcen in this respect since during the struggle for Independence there were not many men who affiliated themselves with the party in a formal way. Most preferred to hedge their bets or maintain their neutrality.

After Independence there was a move by some of the villagers who had been supporters of the French, particularly Mohammed bel Ghazi, to join the Istiqlal party. But when they were allowed to join, many of the original members left in protest; they felt that these new members were merely opportunists trying to redeem themselves—as, of course they were—and they did not want to be in the same party as these latecomers. The urban directors of the Istiqlal party failed to understand these sentiments as they encouraged and allowed everyone to join. Therefore, the membership of the village chapter shifted rapidly from the pro-Independence to the anti-Independence faction. Mohammed bel Ghazi became the head of the Istiqlal in Sidi Lahcen and has held this post since shortly after independence. The sheikh in Zgan also was an Istiqlal supporter of the same type. Although Zgan had also been a pro-French stronghold, the leaders there quickly associated themselves with the Istiqlal after Independence, thus alienating many rural people.

As a reaction to this, some villagers joined two other parties which were formed in the years following Independence. The first and more important in the region was the "Mouvement Populaire," which was formed as a "Berber-rural" party to stand in opposition to the "Arab-urban" Istiqlal. Although these rhetorical characterizations are inadequate, they were used as handles by the villagers themselves; furthermore, the phenomenon of joining the new party to oppose the older one was the main factor at work, at least initially. The original leadership of the Mouvement Populaire in the region came mainly from leaders of the liberation army and later men who, like Ali, had become dissatisfied with Istiqlal. There had been great expectations for Independence, and when little changed there was general disappointment and resentment, some of which was directed against Istiqlal, which in the villagers' eyes had promised much and achieved little.

The third party, with only a minimal following in the village, was the Union National des Forces Populaires (UNFP), a breakaway from Istiqlal whose main strength was in the large industrial centers. With the banning of this party in the early 1960s and the subsequent assassination of its leader, Ben Barka, the party suffered a general decline.

In the early 1960s the leaders of each of the parties in Sidi Lahcen were from the Ait Ghazi ben Allal sublineage. There was Mohammed bel Ghazi for Istiqlal. The leader of the Mouvement Populaire was the moqaddem of the Ait Sidi Hamid lineage. It is interesting to note that while on the national level the UNFP was a left-wing breakaway party from the Istiqlal, in Sidi Lahcen the UNFP drew its support from dissidents from the Mouvement Populaire. The Istiqlal was frowned upon in the village because it was led by Mohammed bel Ghazi and because the sheikh in Zgan was a member. The split in the Mouvement Populaire also came about because some of the villagers felt that the party was not discriminating enough in its membership. Although it was a party supposedly for the Berbers, the support of the wlad siyyed was also explicitly sought. The regional headquarters ordered that they should be included and one of them even accompanied the national secretary on a speaking tour, reading sections of the Koran before he spoke. This strategy of flattering the wlad siyyed worked quite well for a while. But in the mid 1960s there was a scandal in which the party leaders in the region were convicted of stealing party funds, and interest dwindled rapidly after that.

In sum, political activity and interest in national politics and parties were high following Independence, and most of the men in the village affiliated themselves with one of the national parties. Within ten years, interest had dropped to a very low level due to the various local scandals as well as the general depoliticalization which has occurred in Morocco. It became apparent not long after Independence that the parties were not a real source of reward or power, and interest in them and competition for positions decreased correspondingly. Ali, having left the Istiqlal when Mohammed bel Ghazi joined, and having been squeezed out of a leadership position in the Mouvement Populaire by the strategy of choosing a wlad siyyed, was thus unable to find a base for himself and attachment to wider networks here.

Emerging from the period of the fight for Independence—when individual qualities were at a maximum and particular collective affiliations at a minimum—with no institutionalized base of support or power, Ali found himself thrown back on his own resources. Resenting the Ait Ghazi ben Allal people who had taken over the leadership of the political parties, Ali began to attract Berbers from the surrounding areas to his store and he tried to establish a clientele and network of obligations in this way. Further, he cultivated a friendship with the sheikh in Zgan which led to the beginnings of the polarization process within the village. However, after the disaster of the rural commune center, he has not been able to turn this into real support for himself and has been soundly defeated in each election.

The reasons for his losses are interesting because there seemed to be a real potential for the emergence of an alternate power base, with collective support, since almost half the villagers are not wlad siyyed and the village is surrounded by Berber tribesmen. Yet, as we have seen, Ali has never received more than one-tenth of the votes in any election and has also failed to build from the base of his store.The reasons for this failure must be related to his character and personal qualities. He has never been able to build up a real clientele among the Berbers mainly because of his lack of generosity. He is very tight on credit, does not entertain a great deal, and seems almost constitutionally unable to distribute presents. Along with this he has a striking inability to work or cooperate with others. During the fight against the French, when men went out at night alone to do their sabotage work, Ali's qualities were at a premium. Later, qualitites such as generosity, careful calculation, and cultivation of relationships were required, and Ali lacks these.

It seems entirely possible that had Ali been a different sort of person, the direction in which the village has moved would have been significantly altered. Had he been able to mobilize his potential allies and develop a tactic of more tempered and on-going confrontation, he would have had a higher chance of success. This has not happened. Ali continues to play an important role in the village, but a role, it seems, that is likely to diminish. He lacks the personal qualities, the collective backing, and the ties to an external institution or network that are necessary to establish power in Sidi Lahcen. He is likely to spend many years sitting in his store, grumbling.

Chef Abdelkrim—the Moroccans go one way, he goes another. Chef Abdelkrim be Allal of the Ait ben Shedli sublineage has already played and undoubtedly will continue to play a central role in village life. The sources of his importance, the ends toward which it is directed, as well as the confusions it has engendered in him are quite different from those of Ali. They offer an informative comparison on all three counts.

Abdelkrim is the son of a poor and pious man from the Ait ben Shedli (a different branch from Si Jelloul). His rise to prominence resembles that of the qadi Abadi and Si Jelloul in that all three achieved their success by first leaving the village, becoming involved with national networks and institutions, and then returning to the village—or acting on it—after attaining wealth and power in the outside world. For the qadi Abadi and Si Jelloul this entailed attending the Qarawyin, becoming religious judges, and then understanding and pursuing the possibilities opened up by the French support of the Muslim court system. For Chef Abdelkrim, the path which brought him wealth and power was more circuitous. In his generation, the bases of power had shifted and his link to wider networks has been through the army (both French and Moroccan). Along with Ali, but in contrast to Abadi and Jelloul, this itinerary has left him quite confused about his identity. Having achieved great wealth and power—albeit at the loss of his eyesight—he is unsure what power means and how to utilize it, a problem never experienced by the Moqaddem Hamid, Qadi Abadi, or Si Jelloul.

Abdelkrim grew up in Sidi Lahcen, left school early, and became a shepherd and farm worker. This work did not suit him, and when the opportunity arose in 1949 to enlist in the French army he seized it. After training in Meknes, he was shipped off to Indochina (he refers to it as "la Chine"). His army training in Meknes was a highly formative experience for him; the tough discipline of the barracks, the strict chain of command, and the possibility of applying immediate sanctions all combined to form part of a very explicit set of standards he developed to judge both his own conduct and that of his fellow villagers.

The Chef was apparently a fierce warrior and enjoyed the combat in Indochina although he was bewildered by the political dimensions of the war. He questioned me frequently, seeking explanations for "communism," "democracy," etc., in terms of their "big men." He knows political ideology is important but remains unsatisfied with the explanations he has devised.

Toward the end of his year in Indochina, a mortar shell exploded, peppering his skull with large amounts of shrapnel. He vividly remembers the long, arduous trip in a four-engine plane from Hanoi to a hospital in Paris, where he stayed for several months undergoing a series of operations to remove the metal from his skull. At the time it seemed as if he had fully recovered. The stay in the Paris hospital and the treatment he received left a deep impression on him; since the French had given him such excellent care, he could continue to expect it from them and he could count on them; they were indebted to him.

He returned to Sidi Lahcen in 1952, still a young man but greatly changed. He was restless in the village and searched around for projects to undertake. His first scheme was to take over the tobacco franchise from Ali, who had abandoned it when the Istiqlal called for a boycott. The Chef saw this as a chance to make money. Straight ideological arguments, then as now, failed to sway him. The venture, however, proved neither profitable nor sufficiently demanding, and he shortly abandoned it.

The Chef made contact with Qaid Lahcen Lyussi in Sefrou, who personally persuaded him, playing on the possibilities of adventure and camaraderie, to join the liberation army. Although the Chef had just violated the Istiqlal boycott, and was also in the middle of negotiating a business deal which involved Qaid Larbi, he was swayed personally by Lyussi, reversed himself, and joined the liberation army. His reasons were not only the search for action, although that as well as the discipline and rugged manliness of the project certainly appealed to him. He was influenced mainly, it seems, by Lyussi's praise, which flattered him and made him feel part of a national effort, a feeling which is still very important to him. Lyussi offered him wider horizons and important connections. The Chef threw himself whole-heartedly into the fight.

After the stint with the liberation army, he moved to Rabat where he lived from 1955 to 1964. There he joined the newly formed royal army and acquired his nickname "the Chef" because of his rank as adjutant chef. He was stationed near the American base at Kenitra which brought him into frequent contact with the Americans, whose friendliness and generosity deeply impressed him. In contrast to the other villagers, however, the Chef was reluctant to accept the hospitality because it made him feel dependent. But he was fascinated by both the bounty at the base and the casualness of the interaction. He often returned to Kenitra to visit, having bought cigarettes in Rabat at ten times their Post Exchange price; for him this was the demonstration of his independence.

This second set of army experiences—the apparent ease of interaction, the wealth, and the seeming efficiency—were added to his list of absolute standards to be imitated and against which he judges his fellow Moroccans. Reflecting deeply on these experiences—he returns to the theme time and time again in conversation—he became convinced that Moroccans, with the exception of the elite, are inferior barbarians, "tartars." He goes one way, he says, and the Moroccans go another.

Rather unexpectedly, another turning point in his life occurred when one of his officers in Rabat recommended him for the post of chauffeur for the then prince, Moulay Hassan. He was accepted and moved into a house next to the royal compound. During this period he met and was in regular contact with all of the major figures in Morocco including, of course, the king (as the sultan is now called) and the crown prince. He was again overwhelmed by the experience and unsure what role to play. He alternated between two extremes: drinking, whoring, and driving fast cars with his army friends, or attempting to play the young technocrat-sophisticate in Rabat: cruising around wearing sunglasses, smoking a pipe, buying French newspapers and conspicuously displaying them even if he could not read them. He was passionately devoted to Moulay Hassan and listened carefully to what he advised.

Suddenly in 1963 he began to lose his eyesight. His wounds from Indochina had never fully healed. He was shunted from hospital to hospital—Rabat, Paris, Rabat—but nothing could be done and within four years he was totally blind.

Gradually he abandoned hope and came back to Sidi Lahcen. He drank heavily, sat around, collected his pension which, by village standards, was now enormous (total disability plus family assistance), visited Sefrou, Fez, and Immouzer, and tried to decide what to do. Finally, he resolved that he would have to stay permanently in Sidi Lahcen. He had already bought a plot of land from his father when he left the army and had built a house on it. With the assistance and guidance of the farm bureau in Sefrou, the Chef began to buy up large tracts of land, but only land which could be worked with modern methods. The tracts—largely uncleared and uncultivated—were in an area which forms the outer limits of the secondary agricultural land. The distance from the village, the lack of irrigation, and the difficulty of clearing the land, have combined in the past to leave this land fallow.

There is a possibility that a major dam will be built farther up the Sebou river. If this happens, the land will become irrigated farmland. Even if it does not happen, however, the Chef's move is still a good one. In this area he can accumulate large plots inexpensively and quickly in a way he never could in the core area. This enables him to work the land with modern equipment rented from the farm bureau, which also supervises the work. If the dam is not built, the bureau has advised him that with his capital it would be feasible to dig wells and thus irrigate the land. In any case, the Chef has become the biggest land owner in Sidi Lahcen without the endless border problems of the core land and without the entanglements of the village irrigation system. He is a man on his own. The personal gain for him will certainly be large but the implications for the future of the village are equally important.

The limits of possible land expansion have been reached and the population is steadily growing. The Chef has, with his purchases, closed off any possibility of expansion for other villagers, and in the long run this must have important economic effects on village life. The government, as part of an anti-erosion drive in the Middle Atlas, has let it be known that it intends to reactivate its pre-Protectorate rights to a large portion of the secondary land which had at one time been forested. These claims are in abeyance because there was such a strong rural reaction against the program, but the threat that the land may disappear from village control is present. Villagers have therefore refrained from using fertilizer or planting olive trees on the disputed land for fear that it might be confiscated. Meanwhile the Chef will continue to acquire more of the secondary land, as no one can possibly outbid him. There will thus be a definite closing down of possibilities for many families, and a severe squeeze is not unlikely as families lose land to the government—land which they will not be able to replace.

The Chef expresses a complex and contradictory view of the world when he talks about his reasons for buying the land. First, he says, he has a duty to Morocco and to the king. He has heard the king say, both on the radio and in person, that if Morocco is to become a modern country it must modernize its agricultural production. The Chef says that personally he has no need for the land, for he could live quite well from his pension and need not be bothered with all the problems of supervising his workers. He feels, however, that he has an almost personal obligation to the king and he is going to fulfill it. The agricultural bureau has played on this theme and tells him that by modernizing he would serve as a model for other villagers (which because of economic differences is absurd) and help spread modernization. This level of aspiration is not to be underestimated. The Chef's life has been one of extremes, moving from the royal palace to Sidi Lahcen, and his sense of isolation and disorientation is acute. Unable (*kay-heshem bezzef*) to face his former colleagues now that he is blind, he has almost totally retreated from the wider society. By modernizing his agriculture he feels that he is a part of a national effort. This is very important to him.

The sheer activity itself is also vital to him. He has always been a tremendously active man, sleeping only three hours a night. Now he personally supervises all of his workers, despite his blindness, and works his men with a ferocity that is paralleled only by his generosity with them. Moroccans are like donkeys, he says: if you leave them on their own, they will not work.

He uses the farm produce to "ensure himself a government" as he puts it. If you have money, he says, then you have rights, and only then. Consequently, with the farm products as well as the oil and olives from his trees, he makes large and numerous presents to officials in Sefrou. He sells none of his large yield; what he and his merry men do not consume is redistributed. The effectiveness of this policy is clear enough; he has a government. One of his workers was caught stealing a cow in Sefrou. Before arresting him, the gendarmes brought him out to Sidi Lahcen in their jeep to find out if it would be inconvenient for the Chef to have his assistant in jail at that time. At present, the Chef does not have any defined personal or political ambitions; rather, he is insuring his own tranquillity and immunity. He has already built an impressive alliance of networks and obligations; should he ever need them, they are there.

Although the Chef is now protecting the interests of the wlad siyyed, he has very little to do with them. He does not actively engage in local politics. Both the other villagers and the Chef himself say that he would never work with a group of Moroccans on any project. His allegiances are to himself, to the king, and to the country.

Yet his attitude toward the community is a deeply ambivalent one. He has decided to stay in Sidi Lahcen and is keenly interested in village and regional affairs. Further, he provides work to several of the most destitute men, so that they can have some meat occasionally while preserving their dignity. He generously supports the fqi of the mosque, although he never goes to the mosque himself. He will never attend a wedding, circumcision, or funeral, but always sends large gifts.

His attitudes toward Islam are also complex. He does not pray, does not attend the mosque, and has openly broken many basic proscriptions. He constantly insults the pious, mercilessly mocking his father among others, but he definitely conceives of himself as a Muslim. This was dramatically revealed one day during the month of Ramadan when he was particularly edgy (not being able to smoke). Dropping his usual sarcasm about Islam, he launched into a speech about the Koran, proclaiming that it is the most marvelous book ever written and must be impossible to translate because if the Europeans had read it they would have all converted instantly. It is totally true, he claimed, and explains everything. In a fury, he spurred his horse and rode off.

The Chef is a modern version of the old *grand seigneur*. He is terrifying, unchallengeable, and extremely generous. He is impulsive, seemingly unpredictable, and moody, which only adds to his impressiveness and to the fear and respect which he inspires in other villagers. However, the Chef is also a modern man, confused about his world and the place he has in it. He is a loner. One of his favorite expressions is "Les grosses têtes, jamais la-bas"—"Big shots have nothing but trouble." This mixture of French and Arabic exemplifies his frustration in trying to integrate his fragmented, yet intense life. "Big shots," for him, have trouble because Moroccans can never meet his rigorous standards imposed from the outside. But he knows he will have to deal with Moroccans for the rest of his life. Like Si Jelloul and Qadi Abadi and unlike the Moqaddem Hamid or Sidi Lahcen, he is, at best, an ambivalent model for the villagers. They fear and respect his power. But they have no possiblity of imitating him and so they simply watch.

6. The Politics of Culture

Challenge and Doubt

By the early 1960s, partial synthesis and temporary equilibrium had again been achieved in Sidi Lahcen. The village had emerged from twenty tumultuous years with its cultural identity—as rural religious center—weakened but preserved. After the loss of the rural commune, the wlad siyyed handily defeated and kept from office their major opponent, replacing him instead with one of their most trusted and solid representatives. As far as they were concerned, politics was still being carried on in their terms. A time of turning away from the larger regional and national arenas seemed to be in order.

But again, appearances were misjudged. The most effective consensus which seemed to have been won—cultural identity—became the most problematic. That which had seemed the most problematic—socio-economic status—proved to be the area where certain factions and individuals of the wlad siyyed were most successful in consolidating their position.

The wlad siyyed were directly confronted in the late 1960s over their claims to symbolic domination. So far these overt challenges have been parried. On a less obvious level, however, the wlad siyyed have come to doubt themselves and their own worth. This self-doubt was revealed in their behavior during the musem, and it offers us a closing image and theme.

REVOLT OF THE WLAD ABAD

In 1967 the non-wlad siyyed members of the village "revolted" against the wlad siyyed. All the concerned parties were reluctant to discuss the issue. It seems, however, that two young schoolteachers from the wlad abad returned to Sidi Lahcen for their summer vacation and waged a campaign against the wlad siyyed.

Essentially they were working to eliminate the symbolic prerogatives of the wlad siyyed. The teachers worked diligently during the course of the summer at persuading people to join them. Their efforts culminated in a secret meeting during the harvest. It was held late at night when it was natural for groups of men to congregate in the fields. Perhaps fifteen or twenty men, most of them young, attended. Older men were generally excluded since it was known that they considered this activity *hashuma*, inappropriate. In fact, the conspiracy was revealed to the wlad siyyed by an old man from the wlad abad.

The young schoolteachers proposed that the honorific term "Sidi" be dropped. Generally, in Morocco, this term is restricted to shurfa and is a sign of respect, a symbolic recognition of "specialness." The young men argued that the wlad siyyed, as a group, were not superior to anyone else. They agreed that the habits of the older villagers were too deeply engrained to be changed. Even they themselves, they conceded, would find it difficult to alter their ways. Therefore the effort to equalize themselves with the wlad siyyed should be centered on the youth. They proposed that their own children should stop addressing the wlad siyyed as "Sidi." When domination loses its legitimacy, it is experienced as humiliation, even bondage.

There appears to have been general agreement at the meeting, and the following revolutionary plan was adopted: the children of the men present were to deny the recognition of the "specialness" of the wlad siyyed by refusing to call them "Sidi." Further, they were not even to play with the children of the wlad siyyed. After the schoolteachers had left the village to return to work, the revolt was sustained by Ali, who with his nine children was in an excellent position to serve as exemplary leader. He was a vocal, if cautious, critic of the wlad siyyed, as we have seen, and was eager to play the role. His organizational abilities and charisma, however, were low, and so far he has not been very successful. The leadership of the schoolteachers seems to be a necessity. It is unclear how far they are willing to go.

The revolt turned out to be very short-lived in terms of action. At first, the strategy of separating the children occasioned many fights and much consternation and anger among the wlad siyyed. Their moral outrage was shared by the older men from the non-wlad siyyed groups to whom such behavior was truly revolutionary, that is, "unimaginable." The teachers and their supporters were rather quickly isolated and threatened with action by the qaid. The non-wlad siyyed, including Ali, bowed to this pressure and temporarily called off their actions. Obviously this has not resolved the conflict but merely halted the offensive.

The challenge of the schoolteachers has two dimensions, cultural and economic. The future, they reasoned, belongs to the educated classes; only those who do well in school are going to have the security of a government job and assured income. Therefore they would attempt to isolate their children and give them extra tutoring.

Appropriately enough, many young Ait Ghazi bel Allal have become Arabic teachers. The young wlad abad, realizing that the potentiality for growth was much greater elsewhere, have wisely opted for more modern and secular studies. In fact, these wlad abad young men have skirted the cultural monopoly of the wlad siyyed by becoming French-language teachers. All three leaders of the revolt taught French. Although this choice will seemingly bring increased social and economic security to these individuals, it is not likely to have a major effect on village structure.

In response to this explicit challenge, the Chef Abdelkrim and some of the Ait Ghazi ben Allal have decided that no *wlad siyyed* land should be sold to non-shurfa. They have publicly announced that they will buy (cash in hand, in the style of Si Jelloul) any land which is for sale.

The Chef says that originally the *niya*, literally "intention" (character), of the wlad abad was incomplete, *nqsa*, like a half-filled cup of coffee. It improved because they were generous and hospitable to Sidi Lahcen. Now they have lost their land to the wlad siyyed and are fast losing their niya. The young wlad abad have bad niya; they think that their ancestors were crazy for helping Sidi Lahcen. They try to be like the wlad siyyed by studying hard. They think that this will make them just like the shurfa and bring them money and land. The wlad siyyed, says the Chef authoritatively, are going to make sure they are not successful.

Ironically, the economic challenge has been blunted rather more successfully than the cultural one. Many of the young wlad siyyed are now faced with the problem of self-justification. One villager who attends the Qarawiyin University in Fez often discussed questions of Islamic reform with me. He agreed that there were two sources of shurfa-ness: works, *amel*, and genealogy, *nasab*. The true shurfa in Islam, he argued, were the shurfa of works. They should be given recognition and deference because they were exemplary Muslims and led outstanding lives. Each Muslim should be judged on his own worth. None of the older wlad siyyed would concur with this line of argument;

whereas they do not deny works, they staunchly maintain that genealogy is primary.

Once our discussion turned to the subject of the wlad abad revolt, however, the student reversed himself rather dramatically and passionately proclaimed that any wlad siyyed is better than any non-shurfa. He caught himself, realizing what he was saying. In a tone of bewilderment and fear he asked "what there would be," if the position of the shurfa were to be changed. Though he had argued many times against saint worship, once even basing his case on a book of Sidi Lahcen which he had found in Fez, he had never really thought about the implications of his rhetoric.

The dogmatic reaction of the young student indicates that the challenge to the symbols of identity of the wlad siyyed is a deep one. The response so far has been a rigid and angry counterattack. Whereas the older wlad siyyed have reacted out of affront and outrage, it seems that some of the younger men have themselves been torn. Perhaps the symbols of identity and cultural continuity are beginning to lose their hold on them.

The seeds of a profound change in Moroccan culture are germinating. The rise of the genealogical principle and its successful institutionalization occurred at the time of Sidi Lahcen. It is being questioned today. Culture is becoming political again, though the consequences are unpredictable. As any Moroccan farmer will tell you, planting seeds does not mean that they will grow. Growth depends on the climate, good luck, and the blessing of Allah.

THE MUSEM

Twice a year, once in the spring, just before the beginning of the harvest, and once in the fall, after the wheat has been separated from the chaff, a musem or celebration for Sidi Lahcen is held. The musem, at least in principle, is the celebration for which the Ait Yussi contracted with their saint. They are, in fact, central actors at the musem, but the musem is by no means restricted to them. Teams of riders come from factions of the Beni Yarghra, Beni Sedden, Ait Helli, and Ait Seghrouchen, and not all the Ait Yussi themselves participate. Spectators come from the entire region as well as from nearby cities.

When harvest time nears in the spring—the date shifts from year to year because of the tremendous variability of climatic conditions— the moqaddem of the Ait Yussi tours the Ait Yussi of the plain to ascertain the condition of the grain. When he decides that there are two weeks remaining before the beginning of harvesting activity, he informs the qaid in Sefrou, who, after obtaining official permission from the central government, has the musem announced in the local markets. In principle the musem should be held just before the start of the harvest. Because of the timing of the first musem, it is always significantly smaller than the second. The members of the Ait Yussi of the plain are preoccupied with the preparations for the harvest, and some may already have begun harvesting because of the tremendous variation in micro-ecological conditions and the unpredictability of the weather. The Ait Yussi of the mountain are similarly preoccupied, and the often uncertain state of the weather tends to dampen spirits.

The musem in the fall is always much better attended, "full," *ammer* as the expression goes. It comes during a lull after the heaviest work of the year has just been finished, and before the first rains of the fall which may come in a couple of weeks or not for several months. Everyone is free and eager for such festivities. After a good agricultural year, the enjoyment and thanksgiving are enhanced; after a poor year the saint's assistance will be sought.

During the time of siba, the musem was itself a testimony to the religious importance and power of the wlad siyyed and the baraka of the tomb of Sidi Lahcen. The Ait Yussi would reunite twice a year and come to renew themselves: to attain baraka—religious power, divine blessing. The agricultural basis of the musem is clear enough even if this has not been developed in the legend and the interpretation which surrounds it. The Ait Yussi prefer to phrase the reasons for the musem in a different idiom. They say that they come to renew the *dikr*, literally "litany," but here more properly "message" of the saint. They bring offerings, *ziara*, for the saint, hoping that this will bring them his favor. It is a time for the renewal of friendships and pacts, and also of conflict. But this is too general and we must now turn to a closer examination of the style and form of the musem to arrive more directly at its significance.

The form of the musem is as follows: for three days, each of the Berber teams of horsemen—and there is great variation in the number and size of these teams—assembles at one end of a central flat area in the village. Their leader, sheikh, chants a song of praise to the saint that he himself has composed. The song is delivered in a style very similar to that of Koranic chanting but more staccato in its phrasing and more driving in its tone. On a signal from the sheikh, the horsemen charge down the narrow central area, attempting to keep in stride, and then, a few yards before the end of the course, they rein in abruptly, horses rearing, guns firing more or less in unison.

On the first day these songs are usually fairly conventional and consist of direct, standardized praise of Sidi Lahcen's baraka. In the beginning, the audience does not focus its attention on the verses themselves, but as the musem runs its course, they increasingly dominate the event and are the medium through which the tone of the musem is molded and expressed. At first it is rather the singer's style, his delivery, and his cleverness which are acclaimed or castigated by the audience.

Most of the teams are led by one man known as their sheikh, a word which has the dual meaning of singer and chief. He is both the leader of his team and the composer of the songs that exemplify their strength. The team usually comes from a single village where this sheikh is likely to be a "big man."

While the horses are nervously dancing in place, the sheikh chants his laudatory song in taut, highly pitched bursts of sound. The display, style, and demeanor of the performance here is clearly more important than the number of riders, which varies, or their kin affiliation. The Berbers' horses, elegant Arabian stallions fitted with richly decorated saddles, are impressive objects to the villagers, for whom a couple of donkeys are a luxury. Their riders display their most expensive clothes, their gold teeth, as well as western watches as more contemporary proof of their affluence. If bounty is a sign of God's grace in Morocco, and if bounty breeds bounty, then no effort should be spared to exhibit it. The musem is a forum for such display. All who participate—Berber horsemen, the wlad siyyed, and the spectators drawn from near and far—wear their finest clothes and show themselves to their best advantage so as to please the saint and demonstrate their own worth.

The horse display is not a contest, although, as we shall see, competition of a special sort is indeed involved. As the wlad siyyed conceive the scenario, the musem should ideally proceed at a steady level of intensity, rising slightly toward the end of the third day when the musem is fullest with people, displays of bounty, and baraka. In the model situation, the teams would compete in praising the saint and in doing honor to his descendants; they would enjoy themselves, pay their respects, leave gifts, and return to their Berber villages. A good deal of the wlad siyyed's reluctance to admit interest in the musem and their constant derogation of the Berbers stems from the fact that the musem is so structured that it rarely follows this rather placid pattern.

The wlad siyyed try to retain what they think is scholarly decorum, to distinguish themselves from the Berbers who openly enjoy the songs. Although they staunchly attempt to maintain their inability to understand Berber, they usually succumb to the pleasures of the language and the flair of the performances by the middle of the first day. The tension between the competitive singing, and even the musem itself, and the position that the wlad siyyed occupy as men whose baraka has come from a scholarly saint (and who themselves occupied a position of religious teachers and mediators) is, however, present throughout. The wlad siyyed often say that they do not look forward to the musem and that it is really only the Berbers who fully enjoy it. At first this attitude seemed rather condescending since today the wlad siyyed are certainly neither great scholars nor effete urban religious teachers. Further, the festive side of the musem is both a welcome break in the drab day-to-day activity in the village, as well as an explicit recognition of the saint and his descendants. This tension is real enough, however, as are the contradictions which underlie it. The musem is a time of heightened supernatural presence, a dangerous, unstable state which can just as easily bring quick destruction as increased bounty.

The usual form of Berber singing-encounters is agonistic. Form being set, one singer makes up a verse on a given theme and the other singer has to improve the imagery and linguistic possibilities of his opponent's verse. These sessions usually last all night and get extremely caustic as well as uproariously bawdy. Their setting, however, is explicitly profane, and the singers act as individuals. The audience takes pleasure in the virtuoso skill of the poet's handling of the language as much as in the insults which emerge. This same form, however, in the context of the musem takes on different connotations. The musem is explicitly an occasion to honor the saint; the songs which are frowned upon as inherently provocative by the wlad siyyed, are tolerated and enjoyed as long as they stay within the bounds of praise for the saint. Competition for the saint's favors is one thing, however, and antagonistic jousting is quite another. The ongoing repetition puts the whole process under great internal stress to move in more provocative directions. Once the usual forms of praise are exhausted, there is an almost inevitable shift toward denigrating the others. These taunts are not likely to pass by unanswered and the tensions mount.

As the setting of the musem is explicitly conceived as nonantagonistic, the entrance of the extremely profane dimension is considered scandalous, *ayb*. The goal of the musem is to renew the contact with the saint; it is the only time during the year that these groups come together and they do so to praise their patron saint so he will continue to protect them and assure their prosperity.

It is precisely this religious, communal aspect of the setting which underlines and augments the built-in tension of the musem. Times of heightened religious presence and intensity are times of heightened stakes—communal ones in this case. If all goes well, the riders perform well, the musem is full (*ammer*), food is plentiful, gifts to the saint are abundant, pacts are made, friends reunited, and no incidents occur, then the saint will be pleased; all is well and he is virtually coerced into continuing and augmenting this communal well-being. This state of affairs is already proof of his pleasure. The reverse, however, also holds, hence the pervasive wariness and anxiety.

The first day of the musem which I attended passed in much the desired form. It was a modest crowd, with five teams of horsemen drawn from several groups, the chanting of songs of praise by the various sheik-s, and the displays of riding. The mood was an unfocused one, with little explicit antagonism and a general feeling that all was going well. The saint was being praised, reunions were occurring, food was being consumed, and tea was being drunk. The wlad siyyed were anxiously content, almost relieved.

At night there was music, dancing, and lavish feasting. Although the wlad siyyed consider the dancing to be improper, their condemnation is rather more half-hearted—a seconding of views passed on from those in Fez—than heartfelt. This night activity is the one aspect of the musem which the villagers would admit to anticipating with pleasure: good meals, friends, visits, and dancing.

The second day of the musem started out in much the same way as the first. Early in the morning the teams of riders began their rounds of chanting and horsemanship. Shortly after lunch, however, it became apparent that the wlad siyyed were becoming very upset. It was not immediately clear to me what was wrong as the chants were in Berber. Crowd interest was slowly focusing and intensifying at this point; the activity of the whole village changed from a rather casual, dispersed one, in which everyone was alternating daily business with watching the riders, to one in which more and more people started congregating around the participants. An intense singer-audience dynamic was clearly developing. Everyone was making an effort to follow the songs, many villagers receiving running translations from their Berber friends. The pace of this development was unhurried and stretched over several hours in the hot afternoon sun, adding to the mounting uneasiness. It gradually emerged that the two leading sheikh-s were overtly denigrating each other while praising themselves.

Each team, with its sheikh, represents a larger social grouping. Thus, when the sheikh-s turn to antagonistic denigration, it is no longer an individual affair but a group one. A sheikh often begins his attack with references to others from the faction of the opposing sheikh. This brings approval from the audience, and as each faction encourages its sheikh, members of the audience often choose sides and participate on this vicarious level; escalation is almost inevitable. Every effort is made to sway the antagonists back to a more restrained course but once things accelerate, moralistic suasions are unlikely to prevail.

In the musem which I witnessed, the tension continued to build, the horsemen strained to excel, the songs became more and more slander-ous—"your villagers are a bunch of drunks and all you do is whore"—and the crowd reaction, while uniformly enthusiastic, be-came polarized and harsh. The wlad siyyed became frantic: armed fighting had broken out on several occasions in the past—a scandal-ous and dangerous affair, and now events seemed to be heading in that direction. Moral exhortation and threats of supernatural retalia-tion were attempted, but to no avail.

Then, after a long and particularly slanderous poem, one of the riders was thrown and badly trampled by the other horses of his own team. Everyone, riders and spectators alike, rushed down onto the course. Everyone said it must have been Sidi Lahcen who threw the man and that the musem must end instantly. A kind of relief (that things had not gotten worse) and of shamefacedness (that both crowd and riders had behaved so ignobly) was the predominant mood as people abruptly made their preparations to leave.

Once things had gone that far, it was impossible for either team to back down and admit defeat. Only Sidi Lahcen could have ended it without real bloodshed. Afterward, the moqaddem of the Ait Yussi assessed fines on the sheikh-s and their teams to be paid to the saint. A real disaster had narrowly been averted, but the musem had again been a failure; this was a reflection, the wlad siyyed felt, of the general low state of affairs among both the Berbers and themselves.

The musem is a cultural forum for display of bounty and assertion of character in which the various actors attempt to exhibit command and focus the baraka of the saint they have come to celebrate. Ostentatious presentations of wealth, talent, and force are ritualized in the musem. The underlying duality of this rhetoric of demonstra-tion, its inherent uncertainty, lies in the fact that one is trying to demonstrate the possession of the very thing which is being sought—baraka. One exhibits proof of divine favor through exemplification of wealth and force, and one attempts to coerce the continuation and increase of this divine favor through this very exemplification and demonstration. A well-played bluff, if you will.

The goal of the musem is to bring divine favor not only on the individual participants but also on the collectivity. (The very referent of the term collectivity is shifting, complex, and ambiguous.) Further, the very form of the musem is well suited to exemplifying the virtues and dangers inherent in this society's energetic, antagonistic, moralistic, and resiliently realistic style of existence. Cultural unity is sought through the controlled expression of individual self-assertion. The model here is divine blessing through individual glorification within a collective context—"the saint blesses those who bless themselves." The collective context is obviously extremely important. A really successful musem would be one in which many great sheikh-s participated and performed brilliantly, where great numbers of people came, filling the village, bearing many gifts for the saint and his descendants. Then the musem would be truly full of baraka. Aggregate bounty is the goal, and here it is additive and almost literally quantitative; musems are judged comparatively—better than ten years ago, not as good as last year.

Thus the musem can fail to please the saint by not being "full," not exemplifying and presenting this rather particularistic collective bounty and force. On the other side, as we have seen, a large, exuberant, festive audience, and talented, assertive, and narcissistic, evenly matched sheikh-s can also lead to a disastrous conclusion. The very form of the musem—the endless repetition of individual self-glorification, the tension inherent in the sheikh-s' poems, the almost necessary turn from assertion to antagonism—is a very friable one.

If the musem is a celebration of the saint, a collective search for baraka, but one fraught with numerous structural and cultural pitfalls, then it is the task of the wlad siyyed to guide the musem to a successful conclusion. Here, as in their other relations with the Berbers, their role is one of buffer, of repairmen trying to patch up disputes, curb excessive provocation, prevent violence. They anxiously scurry about, trying not to deny forceful assertive character but to channel it, to keep it within bounds, to sap it of its virulence through admonishment, chastisement, and example. Their role is that of host and pious—more often pietistic—witness. They offer a context through which antagonism can be transmogrified into agonistic harmony. They are the descendants of the saint, the guardians of his baraka. They are keenly aware of the potential for failure in the musem and of the destructive potential of the saint. They are also aware of the difficulty of keeping these Berbers away from antagonistic and violent confrontation and moving them, instead, into a dynamic and vital harmony. The power of the resources at their disposal to accomplish this is limited. They too must work with their own force of character and personal presence if they are to succeed. The baraka of the saint remains great, while their own is fading.

The musem leaves one deeply impressed with the on-going vitality of the core religious symbols in Moroccan culture. In basic ways, they obviously still provide a meaningful framework within which new experiences can be partially integrated; cultural continuity still allows for authenticity.

The Berber horsemen have filigreed rifles much as their great grandfathers did, but they also wear gold watches and sunglasses. This is no inchoate mixing of old and new. Both are the substance and expression of wealth and power; the symbol of baraka still provides a frame which gives meaning to both. The drama at the musem I have described was real enough. No one denied that the Berber horsemen were strong and proud nor that when the rider was thrown the musem was over. The weak link in the chain, however, was the wlad siyyed themselves, and their almost paralytic anxiety. They were buffeted around within the symbolic forms of the musem, which still held meaning for the Berbers but in which they could not play their part. Their dilemma was poignant. In the words of Robert Creeley, "The unsure egoist is not good for himself."[1] But lacking baraka, where does one find it?

Toward the end of my stay in Sidi Lahcen word was sent from the government in Rabat that money was being allocated to beautify the musem area. The king was restoring his ties with the wlad siyyed. The flat runway would be cleared and leveled. The space for the spectators would be enlarged. The tomb and mosque would be whitewashed. Increased bus service would be provided for each *musem*. A group of wlad siyyed would go to Rabat to renew the *dahir* or decree of their shurfa-hood. This was all to be done, the ministry told the villagers, for the increased glory of the saint.

The reaction of the wlad siyyed was somewhat unexpected. The wounds of the loss of the rural center had not really been healed, and feelings of keen resentment poured forth. Several men said that the work on the musem area was nothing but a luxury. The musem is only twice a year, and the villagers have to live here all year round. What they need, they all agreed, is work, a road, electricity, and schools. The only enthusiasm I could discern was from several young boys who said that at least there would be some work for them fixing the runway. The qaid had promised that only men from Sidi Lahcen would do the work, and they were happy about this.

The irony of the situation is multiple and its pathos real. Self-consciousness is now quite high in the village (those few who live comfortably in Sefrou tend to be more sentimental about the whole affair). The villagers saw immediately that they would receive several days' wages from the offer and little else. They know full well that money from the king and more tourists will not help them regain a sense of themselves.

They are not against the king nor have they abandoned the saint. But they know now that they must begin moving again, that rejuvenation will not come through stubborn adherence to form alone.

The process has now come full cricle. Sidi Lahcen achieved his credentials by defying the sultan, who in turn strengthened his legitimacy by the political submission of the saint. Today both sides are a little weary—the king seeking legitimacy in the countryside by sponsoring saints' festivals and the wlad siyyed anxiously discontented. What they want from the king—work and land—he cannot give them. What they want from themselves—authenticity—cannot come from the outside. The form of local-level saintly groups and government support of them seems to express a vague echo of earlier days. Internally, it is hollow on both sides. The tension is missing. The sultan is not dominating them politically but is seeking their support through public relations techniques. The wlad siyyed are not seeking legitimation of their charisma through the dahir-s of the Alawite shurfa, but anxiously parrying the sense of the loss of baraka. The galloping tension which the Alawites had harnessed has slowed to an amble. New tensions exist, but forms to understand and express them are only barely emergent.

The wlad siyyed today are not miracle workers, exemplary moral figures, refined religious scholars, active mediators, or even more pious than other Moroccans. Yet they *are* the wlad Sidi Lahcen Lyusi. What this means, and how to be the wlad siyyed, is becoming increasingly problematic. They are still the guardians of the religious symbols. But today they find themselves little more than custodians. They are acutely aware of the great power of the saint and deterioration of their own. The saint is still *shih*, powerful and vital, and they are *ayyan*, weak and enervated.

By misunderstanding their place in a larger and changed world, the wlad siyyed began to lose their baraka. It became an external phantom which they would only pursue in vain. Attempting to bring the baraka of the past into the present, as if it were an object, is futile and alienating. *Baraka* is attributed to manifestations of dynamic force in the world, not to nostalgic reminiscences of that force.

Conclusion

Partiality

A basic anthropological axiom is that significance resides in the whole. We approach an understanding of a situation—in my view—by examining the historical interrelatedness of cultural symbols in the context of the social, economic, and ecological orders. A successful anthropological explanation, therefore, cannot eliminate either the historical (which also implies a broader geographical dimension), the cultural, the social taken broadly, or, most importantly, their interconnections. If significance resides in the whole, the reification of any of these realms into an object of study *sui generis* results in a myopic view.

The particular direction of an inquiry follows certain guiding ideas ("man formulates meaning through public symbols," or "social processes escape those who undertake them," etc), but these guiding ideas are neither ends in themselves nor sufficient explanations for anthropology. Rather they are heuristic directions for interpreting specific material. If they become reified into *a priori* constituitive schema, they turn into methods which amount to intellectual terrorism. Their main purpose then becomes to force events, persons, and acts into the prefabricated molds which have been produced for them by the observer. As Sartre says about the Marxists (but it applies equally well to many schools within anthropology): their "aim is not to integrate what is different as such, while preserving for it a relative autonomy, but rather to suppress it."[1] The remedy for this is not to refuse to approach problems in general terms, but to seek particularity within that general context. "It is impossible to deduce the concrete from the general or to dissolve the concrete in the general,"[2] but the concrete by itself is, of course, meaningless.

Specifically, meaning is not found on the cultural level alone but in the partial and imperfect relation of symbols to the particular historical conditions in which they are situated. Particularly where the cultural symbols change more slowly than the social and political order, significance is discovered by examining the concrete inter-dependencies between these orders as they occur in historical develop-ment. Although I have been concerned with the interpenetrations of cultural categories and social processes, the bulk of the narrative has been devoted to an exploration of the shifting conceptions of religion and politics within the social order which has supported or under-mined them. Whereas the two sets of terms—cultural categories and social processes, politics and religion—have been rhetorically bal-anced, one of my major assertions is that the symbolic formulations which are the vehicles of meaning changed much less rapidly than did the material conditions. The basic symbols—conceptions of saintli-ness, mediation, strength, generosity, bounty—have demonstrated an impressive continuity, whereas the material conditions varied in accordance with the tumultuous changes in Moroccan history. Basic new orderings in these realms seem to have emerged almost every generation during the twentieth century. Social conditions and the cultural categories which inform them do not change at the same rate, and this is a source of both the continuity and profound malaise and disharmony in Moroccan society.

This is not meant as a general law. There is no reason to believe that cultural change should always take the form which I have described for the village of Sidi Lahcen. There certainly are situations in which cultural change occurs more rapidly than social alteration; the Third World is full of such examples. Nor does it necessarily even hold for all of North Africa. In my view this is not because it is an inadequate formulation. Rather, this is the nature of social science inquiry. I am not looking for universal structures of the mind, determinative laws of economic development, or middle-range abstractions. As stated ear-lier, this is an actor-oriented approach, one that seeks to understand and make comprehensible the sense of a particular lifeworld. By doing this, one hopes to increase the understanding of other such situations, but not directly through deductive operations. Other instances of change and dissonance may be better analyzed through an understand-ing of Sidi Lahcen, remote as it may seem from us. Such an analysis would suggest that symbols of identity and political movements fuse, clash, and have consequences for economic development. But one would not necessarily expect to find the same constellation somewhere else. There is no possibility of mechanical translation from case to case. But there is the possibility that the proliferation of such studies will reformulate questions, and that the complexity of answers will give rise to a more subtle and penetrating activity.

Anthropology is a humanistic discipline and a science. But it is a dialectic science of reflection whose advancement (obviously not inevitable) consists in the expansion and deepening of its discourse. At its most abstract level, this discourse is between cultures, but concretely it is between a specific researcher and the people of a particular culture. We must remember, of course, that a researcher can be outside a group only to the degree that he is inside another.[3] Since the condition of both the subject and the object are historically located, knowledge is only possible through successive mediations. The mediations, however, must be retained or all is lost. The aim of anthropology is the comprehension of others in order to return, changed, to ourselves.

Notes

INTRODUCTION

1. For an elaboration of some of these ideas see: Joseph Levenson, *Confucian China and Its Modern Fate* (Berkeley and Los Angeles: University of California Press, 1968): Jean Duvignaud, *Change at Shebika: Report From a North African Village* (New York: Pantheon Books, 1970).

2. My theoretical orientation is drawn most obviously from the work of Clifford Geertz, Jean-Paul Sartre, and Max Weber. See in particular: Clifford Geertz, *The Interpretation of Cultures* (New York: Basic Books, 1973); Jean-Paul Sartre, *Critique de la raison dialectique* (Paris: Editions Gallimard, 1960); Max Weber, *Economy and Society*, 3 vols. (New York: Bedminster Press, 1968).

CHAPTER ONE

1. The tension between the two sources of power and authority is ever-present, and the important leaders in Morocco have drawn on both.

2. They also conquered Spain and most of North Africa.

3. Directly this meant Portugal and Spain, but the diplomatic maneuvering involved the other large powers.

4. Jean Brignon et al., *Histoire du Maroc* (Paris: Hatier, 1967) p. 175.

5. Clifford Geertz, *Islam Observed* (Chicago: University of Chicago Press, 1971), p. 30.

6. This status had to be accepted by the local community as well. See chapter 6.

7. George Drague, *Esquisse d'histoire religieuse du Maroc* (Paris: J. Peyronnet & Cie., n.d.), p. 129.

8. Ibid., p. 133.

9. Ibid., p. 190

10. Jacques Berque, *Al-Youssi: Problèmes de la culture marocaine au XVIIième siècle* (Paris: Mouton & Cie., 1958).

11. Ibid., p. 12.

12. Ibid., p. 37.

13. Ibid., p. 84.

CHAPTER TWO

1. Today several young Arabic teachers from the village are familiar with the historical account. Most of Al-Youssi's treatises on logic were too difficult for them to follow. Little embellishment has resulted from their inquiry. They claim to have found proof that Al-Youssi is a degenerate form of Al-Youssifi, which would authenticate the claims to Arab descent put forward on his behalf. These exceptions only reinforce the discussion in this chapter.

2. Edward Westermarck, *Ritual and Belief in Morocco*, 2 vols. (New Hyde Park, N.Y.: University Books, 1968), 1:35–262.

CHAPTER THREE

1. Bernard Hoffman, *The Structure of Traditional Moroccan Rural Society* (The Hague: Mouton & Cie., 1967), p. 21.

3. Ibid., p. 109.

4. E. Aubin, *Le Maroc d'aujourd'hui* (Paris: Armand Colin, 1912).

5. Ibid., p. 244.

6. Jacques Berque, "Qu'est-ce qu'une tribu nord-africaine?" in *Eventail de l'histoire vivante—Hommage à Lucien Febvre* I (Paris, 1953), pp. 260–71.

CHAPTER FOUR

1. Until the *siba* period, families who settled in Sidi Lahcen seem to have been absorbed under the common name of *wlad abad*. That is, all of the various families in the wlad abad claim to have been in Sidi Lahcen for very long periods of time but do not claim common descent. During siba a large number of new families settled in the village; these families have been differentiated from both the wlad abad and wlad siyyed. They have neither common hearths nor identity. They came accidentally—a wandering salesman who was stranded in Sidi Lahcen during severe rains and who returned with his family to live in the village—or on purpose—several Berber families who moved into the village during the siba period to afford themselves the protection of the saint. In general, these families have had a rather difficult time establishing themselves economically in the village. Many have little or no land and work as sharecroppers. It is important to emphasize the number and diversity of these groups. The village has had a fluid social history. It is for this reason that I mention them here. They have not been central actors in the village history.

CHAPTER SIX

1. Robert Creeley, *For Love* (New York: Charles Scribner's Sons, 1962), p. 30.

CONCLUSION

1. Jean-Paul Sartre, *Search For A Method* (New York: Vintage Books, 1963), p. 48.
2. Ibid., p. 102.
3. Ibid., p. 76.

Index

Abadi, the *qadi*, 56–58
Ait ben Shedli (sublineage), 51, 53, 55, 59. *See also* Chef Abdelkrim; Jelloul, Si
Ait Ghazi ben Allal (sublineage), 51, 52, 55, 61; provide political leadership, 76–77; respond to *wlad abad* challenge, 87. *See also* Ghazi, Mohammed bel; Moqaddem Hamid
Ait Helli (tribe), 34–36, 38; and *musem*, 88
Ait Seghrouchen (tribe), 34, 75; and *musem*, 88
Ait Yussi (tribe): *bled* of, 38; celebrate *musem*, 17, 88–89; choose a patron saint, 28; negotiate with Sidi Lahcen Lyussi, 20; pre-Protectorate role of, 34; and Moqaddem Hamid, 42; as seen by the *wlad siyyed*, 39; share common name, 37; Sidi Lahcen Lyussi as religious center, 18
Alawites. *See* Sultans, Alawite
Ali (non-*wlad siyyed* leader), 69, 72–78
Alienation, 1–4
Assal: defined, 38; *wahed*, 29; of *wlad abad*, 39, 53. See also *Qbila*
Aubin, E., 32, 34
Ayyan: baraka as, 29, 66, 96; as opposed to *shih*, 65

Baraka, 2, 18, 25–30, 90, 93–95, 97; defined, 25; of Moqaddem Hamid, 41–43, 64; personal, 24, 27, 48; of place, 25–26; of Sidi Lahcen Lyussi

(saint), 17, 19, 27, 28, 48, 90; transmission of, 8, 18–19, 91; of *wlad siyyed*, 3, 18, 96
Beni Saddan (tribe), 34–36
Beni Warain (tribe), 34, 35, 37
Berbers, 42, 44, 77, 78; celebration of *musem* by, 3, 89–95; as distinct from Arabic speakers, 29, 32, 39; French view of, 32; Islam contemporary for, 3, 95; resistance to French by, 41; unite Morocco, 5; of Zgan, 34, 35, 73. *See also* Ait Yussi
Bled, 20, 29; of Ait Yussi, 38; defined, 27–28; *l-makhzen*, 31, 32, 36, 37; *s-siba*, 31, 32, 36, 37; as territory, 19
Brotherhoods, Sufi, 5, 6, 10–15, 18

Charismatic authority, 7, 23–25, 96; in conflict with genealogical transmission of authority, 7, 8, 12, 30; and political and religious movements, 5. *See also* Maraboutic Crisis
Chef Abdelkrim, 74, 79–83, 87
Commune councils, rural, 72–74
Creeley, Robert, 95

Domination: and *bled*, 27; and imperialism, 2; and *mul*, 28; through submission, 26; by sultans, 25, 37; symbolic, by government, 34; symbolic, by the *wlad siyyed*, 25, 85, 86; symbolic, legitimized in the legend of Sidi Lahcen Lyussi, 18, 23, 24, 34